The Simple Art of Marrying Food and Wine

The Simple Art of Marrying Food and Wine

Photographs by Jason Lowe

MITCHELL BEAZLEY

The Simple Art of Marrying Food and Wine

by Malcolm Gluck and Mark Hix

First published in Great Britain in 2005 by Mitchell Beazley,
an imprint of Octopus Publishing Group Ltd,
2–4 Heron Quays, London E14 4JP

ISBN 1 84533 079 X

A CIP record for this book is available from the
British Library

Set in Din

Colour reproduction by Bright Arts, Hong Kong
Printed and bound in China by Toppan Printing
Company Limited

Photographs by Jason Lowe

Commissioning Editor Hilary Lumsden
Executive Art Editor Yasia Williams
Managing Editor Juanne Branquinho
Editor Vanessa Kendell
Home Economy Assistant Kevin McFadden
Prop Stylist Sue Rowlands
Index Laura Hicks
Design Grade Design Consultants, London
Production Jane Rogers

How to Use this Book

PAGE COLOUR AND SEQUENCE:

White pages - Mark Hix, each of his dishes explore alternative
ingredients or cooking styles in the ingredient boxes found at
the foot of each of the recipe pages.

Tint pages - Malcolm Gluck, his vinous analysis of Mark's
dishes also includes comments on the ingredient boxes in
terms of how they influence the wine chosen, except for where
he adequately covers these aspects in his main text.

WINE CHECKLISTS:

These offer a quick list of the relevant wine styles and their
regions of production, rather than the specific producer
names, which are discussed in greater depth in the main text.

METRIC CONVERSIONS FOR THE USA

Capacity

1 millilitres = ⅕ teaspoon

5 ml = 1 teaspoon

15 ml = 1 tablespoon

30 ml = 1 fluid oz.

100 ml = 3.4 fluid oz.

240 ml = 1 cup

1 litre = 34 fluid oz.

1 litre = 4.2 cups

1 litre = 2.1 pints

1 litre = 1.06 quarts

1 litre = 0.26 gallon

Contents

"...he took care to include a yard of long French bread, a sausage out of which the garlic sang, some cheese which lay down and cried, and a long straw-covered flask containing bottled sunshine..." The Rat's picnic in *The Wind in the Willows*, Kenneth Grahame, 1908.

SO TWO DIVORCED MEN SHOULD REVEAL HOW TO ACHIEVE THE PERFECT MARRIAGE? Life throws up more bizarre anomalies. Perhaps it was our love of food and wine which caused the break-ups. If so, then we have sacrificed a lot to get where we are and you might find it useful to listen.

Years ago the perfect marriage was easy to arrange. The world was strictly divided, culinarily speaking, along ethnic lines, and those few individuals who drank wine with their food chose a bottle either from the region they lived in or from one of a dozen wine-producing countries. The food prepared then was plainer, more sober in appearance, and so were the wines. Grilled sole? You clicked your fingers and a bottle of Chablis arrived. Roast beef? Up from the cellar came a dusty bottle of claret. Dessert? Well, it had to be a Barsac or a Sauternes.

The good old days they may have been, but they were, compared with now, the good old boring days. The world now drinks wine not just from the usual suspects in Europe, but from California, Australia, South Africa, New Zealand, South America, eastern Europe, north Africa... and forty or more other countries. Alongside this wonderful burgeoning in the growth and versatility of the vine has come the incredible diversity and racial cross-over of food ingredients. You can visit any number of restaurants in any of the world's major cities, from Auckland to San Francisco, and be offered a starter with Thai spicing, a main course influenced by Moroccan cuisine, and a pudding with a Japanese provenance. A cookbook written by an Australian may well call upon ingredients of Bangladeshi origin with techniques from Szechuan in China.

We are more aware of what others eat than at any time in human history, and never have we shown such interest in the subject. More of us are familiar with food styles with their dazzling range of ingredients, and we all seem to be eating out more. Magazines, TV, and cookery books spread the word, whether it be how to boil an egg or urging us to go and pick our own wild herbs and mushrooms. We have the means

taught (or embarrassed to admit it). Asian food has hit the streets big time, and we no longer struggle to find herbs and spices to knock up a home-made Thai green curry from scratch. We are fussy about what olive oil we keep in our larders, and some of us keep several types for different culinary uses.

> Finding the right wines for today's dishes is far from straightforward. This book is an attempt to offer a way through this maze of food and wine.

The result of so much choice is an increase in our inventiveness. Supermarket aisles are stretching ever wider and deeper to accommodate new food trends, organics, and, it must be noted, food and drink pairings (not always successfully). As a result of this delicious revolution in taste, the perfect marriage has never been more difficult, never so challenging a prospect. Finding the right wines for today's dishes is far from straightforward. It is fraught with difficulties, and the choices are seemingly endless. Cooking is now an exhilarating, topsy-turvy ride, and so the wines which must be found to accompany such an approach have to be equal to it. Luckily, the wines on offer provide a choice which is deeper and richer than ever before. However, paradoxically (or perhaps inevitably), such an abundance of choice means there is also greater opportunity for confusion.

This book is an attempt to offer a way through this maze of food and wine, where it is so easy to get lost. Travelling to so many of the world's vineyards, as one of us has done, has provided an insight into the food and wine pairings the winemakers themselves enjoy and that are often a revelation to the rest of us (such as New Zealand Sauvignon Blanc with sushi, and South African Pinotage, a red wine, with grilled fish). It is these New World wines which have opened up the diner's horizons and made this book so enticing in its ideas, exciting in its prospects. So many of these modern wines are better suited to the kinds of foods we now enjoy all over the world. The wines of Chile, the Pacific states of the USA, South Africa, Australia, and New Zealand, as well as the increasing number of New World-style wines from Europe, have given us marriage partners aplenty to consider. Critically, however, there is insufficient attention paid to this aspect of wine criticism, just as too many restaurant reviewers fail to discuss the wine list.

Marriage is dead, saith the cynic? Not for the authors of this book. It might be under threat as a social institution, but, for the cook, the diner out, the entertaining and thoughtful host, it is an important, not to say totally defining, union.

It was Maurice Chevalier who so artfully pointed out that, "Many a man falls in love in light so bad he wouldn't choose a suit by it", and so it is that many a wine critic

judges a wine in conditions inappropriate for making choices about its marriage with food. As candidates for partnering with food, wines in a professional wine tasting are given no chance to demonstrate their suitability. Wine is not created solely to be compared with other wines and spat into metal buckets or ceramic spittoons. Wine is made to accompany food. The wine taster must use imagination and skill to speculate on this area, and many critics find they have enough on their plates coming to a simple decision about whether a wine has faults, let alone immediately thinking of what food it best suits. In this regard, it is undoubtedly true that the wine taster's job is made even more intense and complex nowadays owing to all the different kinds of ethnic food referred to above. Old-style European wines do not accompany many modern, ethnically-influenced foods as purposefully as New World wines.

Sometimes, as the following anecdote will illustrate, a sommelier has a problem with marriage. This is what happened to one of us in a fancy London restaurant when the wine ordered, a very young Chinon newly arrived on the list (and one of the cheapest wines on it), seemed to affront the sommelier.

Sommelier (a Frenchman in his prime): *Oh zir. Too zung to drink I tink. Do zu know zis wine? Could I suggest someting else?*

MG: *Do you know what I am proposing to eat?*

Sommelier: *...'er...'erm...*

MG: *I will tell you. I am having the kidneys. They will be pink. That wine will go splendidly with them, because the blood will harmonise with the tannins, just as the pepperiness of the Cabernet Franc grape will go with the gaminess of the meat.*

> Wine is not created solely to be compared with other wines and spat into metal buckets or ceramic spittoons. Wine is made to accompany food.

This restaurant was not, of course, one within Mark's remit. Nor was the place where a roast sea bream with roasted fennel was ordered along with a Barbaresco. The wine waiter demurred at this choice. However, Barbaresco, made like Barolo from the Nebbiolo grape in northwest Italy, is a light but rich red wine with a subtle edging of licorice that works brilliantly with fish and fennel. What this should reveal is that this book has not been slung together over a few good meals. It has been a long time in the researching, and we hope you find the fruits of these delicious labours worth the time to contemplate and, in the case of the recipes, try out. *Vive le mariage parfait!*

1
Vegetables

THE POOR OLD VEGETABLE OFTEN GETS NEGLECTED AND ENDS
UP AS A BIT OF AN AFTERTHOUGHT ON THE DINNER TABLE. You
may as well forget vegetables if you are not going to take good care
of them in both the preparation and cooking stages. How many
times has a restaurant served you sloppy, under- or overcooked
vegetables with no seasoning? I quite like the Spanish approach
where they just don't serve any side orders of vegetables; they're
simply integrated into the starter or main course.

We are not just talking peas and carrots here, though. There are
some amazing vegetables out there which we tend to forget about
that make fantastic stand-alone meals. When I have a dinner party
at home and there are vegetarians present, I will take the
opportunity to make the whole meal vegetarian. It's not as taxing as
it may sound. We have so many great vegetables available to choose
from these days, and shopping for them in supermarkets, farmers'
markets, and specialist greengrocers can be an adventure.

I might open my vegetarian meal with a starter of clear jellied
gazpacho, followed by a wild asparagus risotto, then perhaps a

salad of baby artichokes, and finally a plate of ceps roasted with wild garlic leaves and monk's beard (or *agrette* as it is known in Italian). You see, not a mention of a French bean, a carrot or a petit pois. Now *there's* a great vegetable that has been downgraded by its frozen and canned counterparts. Nothing wrong with frozen peas, you know. In fact, I prefer them to the fresh sort most of the time. You know they are always going to be green, sweet, and tender, and if you are making pea soup or posh mushy peas, then it's pointless podding fresh peas that are going to end up in the blender.

There are some amazing vegetables out there that make fantastic stand-alone meals... gazpacho, wild asparagus risotto, roasted ceps with garlic leaves...

If you are a follower of the seasons, which can be confusing, you will have learned how to appreciate the fact that each of the seasons yields different types of vegetable, which is nature's way of ensuring we have enough variety, and that we can happily munch our way through the year until our favourite crops re-appear. But, without contradicting what I've just said, there are some of the basics that we just can't do without, like good old onions and carrots. These form the basis of stocks and sauces and are used as a trivet for roasting joints of meat on. I suppose because they are so common they get used and abused, and rarely sit at the table on their own. One of my favourite seasonal vegetables is mushrooms, and being a bit of a forager I just can't resist getting into the woods when the season kicks off. In the UK, the season begins on St George's Day, April 23, and you can pretty much pick your way through until the frosts arrive. If you live by the sea there are also opportunities to forage for wild sea vegetables like samphire, from June, and sea beet and sea purslane.

But back to the subject of matching vegetable dishes and wine: I cooked a course at a restaurateurs' dinner a few months back, and confused the hell out of the wine supplier, who was trying his hardest to marry a wine to my white asparagus and artichoke salad with truffle dressing. Over to you, Malcolm.

VEGETABLES AND WINE DON'T SOUND RIGHT TOGETHER. Abbott and Costello, on the other hand, are perfect; Fred and Ginger likewise. But ginger and butternut squash and wine? Nope. Sorry, can't contemplate (or so it seems). Yet we don't shy away from wine and cheese (some people throw parties in their joint honour). We do not guffaw at the prospect of red wine and meat (or poultry), or even red wine with fish. We also go so far as to nominate wines to go with desserts.

But the idea of any sort of wine and vegetable together grates. They appear as uneasy bedfellows in many people's minds, because vegetables are considered an accompaniment to a more expensive, more impressive ingredient. Vegetables are just a bit on the side, and who marries a wine with a bit on the side?

If you are ignorant of the dish's height, weight, leg measurement, and inches around the chest, you will be unable to tailor a wine to fit.

This is to misunderstand the versatility of vegetables and their often central role. There are wonderful cuisines, such as those of the Indian sub-continent, for example, wholly based on vegetables. So, do we then say that such dishes do not deserve wine, or no appropriate wines exist with which to pair them? I would not only argue against this view but would also point out that such exquisite foods often require more careful consideration by the wine waiter than better-known offerings. This is because they are usually subtly rather than aggressively spiced, and more delicate (even when char-grilled or roasted) in flavour and texture. Wines can, therefore, unless chosen with flair and care, overwhelm them.

Vegetables are also not like fish or meat, which can be used, to some extent, to point the wine waiter's way to the perfect wine. Many a vegetable in one dish is as different from its close relative (even twin) in another as Kent chalk is from Mongolian cheese.

Imagine enquiring what wine goes with rice? Okay, fine. But is that sushi you have in mind? Risotto? Fried rice? Pilau, perhaps? You have to be dish-specific. Indeed, I think it is difficult when considering rice to find another central ingredient which can command such a vast repertoire of wines. Beef dishes, for example, or most fish ones, offer a much smaller retinue of wines which serve the purpose of matching them.

In the wines I have chosen for the vegetable dishes which follow, you will note how specific I have had to be. A wine to go with tomatoes? No! A wine to accompany balsamic vinegar and prosciutto. A wine for squash? Oh, dear me, no. A wine which will not take fright at ginger. The broad beans? And cauliflower? The wines have been chosen on the basis of their steadfastness in the face of garam masala, cumin, mustard seeds, and curry leaves. The principle that emerges from this, then, is one that runs throughout this book. Just as you cannot tailor a suit for anyone on the basis of merely knowing his waist measurement, you cannot find a wine to fit a dish if you know only what seems to be the dish's most prominent ingredient, and this is not always the one which the dish is built around. If you are ignorant of the dish's height, weight, leg measurement, and inches around the chest, you will be unable to tailor a wine to fit it.

Slow-baked Plum Tomatoes

SERVES 4

SLOW BAKING IS A GOOD WAY OF USING UP EXCESS TOMATOES YOU HAVE GROWN, OR CHEAP ONES YOU HAVE BOUGHT FROM THE MARKET. Once they are cooked and semi-dried like this, you can preserve them in olive oil with thyme, oregano, or basil in sterilized, Kilner-type jars with a rubber seal (or an airtight container kept in the refrigerator). Use them chopped or blended into pasta sauces. This makes a good starter, antipasti dish, or side dish. You can serve it with a few leaves of rocket or similar salad leaves as a starter.

10 MEDIUM-SIZED PLUM TOMATOES | 2TBSP OLIVE OIL, PLUS EXTRA FOR GREASING | 2TSP CHOPPED THYME LEAVES | 1TSP SEA SALT | FRESHLY GROUND BLACK PEPPER
TO SERVE
3TBSP OLIVE OIL | ½TBSP BALSAMIC VINEGAR | A FEW ROCKET LEAVES (OPTIONAL) | 8 SLICES OF PROSCIUTTO OR GOOD-QUALITY HAM (OPTIONAL)

1. Preheat the oven to 130°C/250°F/Gas mark ½. Halve the tomatoes, cutting through the core. Lay them, cut side up, on a baking tray lined with lightly oiled greaseproof paper. Mix the olive oil, thyme, sea salt, and black pepper, and brush or spoon over the tomatoes.

2. Bake for about 1½–2 hours until the tomatoes have shrunk to half their size and are lightly coloured and caramelized on top. Remove and leave to cool a little.

3. To serve, mix the olive oil with the vinegar and season. If using rocket leaves, place a few onto plates or a large serving dish and arrange the tomatoes on top. Lay the prosciutto on the side and spoon the dressing over.

VINEGAR

When I was a kid, vinegar was Sarson's at the local chippie, which helped to digest the soggy, greasy chips. Now, we are spoilt for choice. White wine vinegar gets left on the shelf for superior and upmarket vinegars from Spain such as Chardonnay and Cabernet Sauvignon. They are more expensive, but they are a foodie's must-have in the larder. Balsamic vinegar hit the streets big time some years back along with its Italian sidekick, the sun-dried tomato, and together they dominated restaurant and dinner party menus. Chefs went mad over it and discovered the art of drizzling thick, aged balsamico on anything they could, including desserts.

Considering vinegar was discovered by mistake, it hasn't done badly in the culinary world. I mean, what would we do without it? Salads would be bland as hell, and pickled onions just wouldn't exist.

SLOW-BAKED PLUM TOMATOES

THE ACIDITY OF TOMATOES WILL NORMALLY TAKE THE EDGE OFF ANY RED WINE, but this dish has its own edge mollified by the prosciutto. Thus, a chilled north Italian Pinot Nero will suit, as will a Valpolicella Classico from Verona (where Shakepeare's most star-crossed pair of lovers are to be found). But a young, chilled Pinotage from the Cape is also good, as are certain New Zealand Pinot Noirs: Mount Difficulty, Ata Rangi, Cloudy Bay, Jackson Estate, Wither Hills, and Villa Maria Reserve, for example. However, in circumstances where the tomatoes in this dish still display some raw acidity the Pinotage is much to be preferred to any Pinot Noir. Names to look for in particular are Clos Malverne, Warwick, Spice Route (which has a particularly funky, gamey edge suited to the dish), and Kanonkop.

It is important to remember that tomatoes are a fruit, not a vegetable, and this implies a degree of acidity. True, cooking will smooth the edge of the acidity away, and in sauces, for example, the fruit is transformed. However, is there any dish with the addition of tomato you can think of in which the acid of the fruit is not a factor in how the food tastes? I exempt from this question salads or antipasto dishes where the tomatoes are raw (in which case a nicely chilled Riesling, from Australia's Clare Valley, Alsace, or the Pfalz or the Nahe in Germany, is required). Tomatoes are acidic, and the wine chooser must take account of this fact. Unless fresh tomatoes are boiled, as in a soup, and cream and herbs are added, they almost invariably retain something of their character – their bite.

WINE CHECKLIST

PINOT NERO (NORTHEAST ITALY)

VALPOLICELLA CLASSICO (VERONA – NORTHEAST ITALY)

PINOTAGE (SOUTH AFRICA)

PINOT NOIR (NEW ZEALAND)

WINE AND VINEGAR
The word vinegar is derived from sour wine. It is no friend of any wine, though Retsina from Greece can cope with it in small doses. In salads, try lemon juice instead to match the wine, but best of all, a crisp dry white wine like Riesling can be utilized instead of vinegar.

Clear Jellied Gazpacho

SERVES 4

GAZPACHO VARIES FROM REGION TO REGION, and is probably Spain's best-known contribution to gastronomy. The original version, *ajo blanco*, was of Moorish origin and contained garlic, almonds, bread, olive oil, vinegar, and salt. When tomatoes were discovered in the conquest of South America, they were added to the soup. Peppers and cucumber joined in later, and it became the dish we know now. Although I love the original, this is a nice, refined version that's slightly removed from its parent but had a good education.

200ML (7FL OZ) TOMATO JUICE | 6 LARGE RIPE PLUM OR ROUND TOMATOES, ROUGHLY CHOPPED | 2½ RED PEPPERS, SEEDED AND ROUGHLY CHOPPED | ½ SMALL ONION, ROUGHLY CHOPPED | ⅔ CUCUMBER, PEELED AND ROUGHLY CHOPPED | 1 SMALL CLOVE GARLIC, CRUSHED | 1TBSP WHITE WINE VINEGAR | ½TSP CUMIN SEEDS | GOOD PINCH OF SWEET PAPRIKA | SALT AND FRESHLY GROUND WHITE PEPPER | 3 LEAVES OF GELATINE
FOR THE GARNISH
½ RED PEPPER, SEEDED AND FINELY DICED | 2 TOMATOES, SKINNED, SEEDED, AND FINELY DICED | ⅓ CUCUMBER, SEEDED AND FINELY DICED | 2TSP CHOPPED CHIVES | 1TBSP OLIVE OIL

1. The day before, put the jelly ingredients, except for the seasoning and gelatine leaves, into a bowl, reserving 50ml (2fl oz) of the tomato juice. Cover with clingfilm, and leave in the refrigerator overnight. Coarsely blend the ingredients in a blender or food processor and season.

2. Line a colander with double muslin or a clean tea towel and place over a large bowl. Pour the tomato pulp into the colander and leave overnight in the refrigerator to drain. The next day you should have about 600–700ml (1–1¼ pints) of clear juice in the bowl.

3. Soak the gelatine leaves (you may need another leaf if you have more like a litre of juice) in cold water until soft. Meanwhile, remove a small ladleful of the juice and heat it in a pan. Squeeze the water from the gelatine leaves and stir them into the hot tomato juice until dissolved. Don't boil it. Add this to the rest of the juice, add the previously reserved tomato juice, and stir well. Put into bowls, giving it a stir or light whisk to break it down, and place in the refrigerator for 1–2 hours until set. Mix the garnish ingredients together, spoon over the top or mix in, and serve.

PEPPERS

Hot and spicy, sweet and nutty – peppers come in many guises. Our translation of pepper generally refers to the sweet red variety. But the colours are many: orange, yellow, green, and black. My preference is the reds, not raw, but roasted until charred, then skinned. This method brings out the sweetness, and you can serve them alone, or with some crumbled goat's cheese or some topnotch anchovy fillets.

It's amazing how the flavour is transformed once they are cooked. I've never been a raw pepper fan – unless it comes in the form of a gazpacho, that is. Peppers tend to get abused in their raw form and are chopped and thrown into salads just to give a bit of colour and crunch. Supermarkets are now selling the elongated sweet ramero peppers that lend themselves perfectly to grilling or roasting, and are great as a starter.

CLEAR JELLIED GAZPACHO

THE PERFECT WINE, WELL CHILLED, FOR THIS CHARMING SOUP IS MANZANILLA – THE SHERRY FROM SANLUCAR DE BARRAMEDA. The tanginess of the soup and the saline richness of the wine make a lovely marriage, one which seems ordained by a higher authority than that scurvy knave of a wine writer. Manzanilla is a fino sherry, one of the wine world's greatest curiosities (rather like Robert Parker, though much easier and less bewildering to swallow). Now, fino owes its individuality wholly to the local yeast, called *flor*, which encrusts the wine and gives it that oxidized, weirdly vegetal, almost as dry as Lapsang tea leaves, undertone. Fino, however, is a product of the town of Jerez (which the English, unable to get their tongues around when it was correctly pronounced as "*hair-reth*", transliterated into sherry), but Manzanilla is a littoral fino from Sanlúcar de Barrameda. As a result of the sea breezes and the humid conditions of the bodegas (cellars), the *flor* is different and the wine has more stridency and pungency. We need both for this soup, which, though delicate in conception, is rather robust, as a sum of its parts, on the palate. However, we can find other candidates for it. Try Barbadillo or Javier Hildalgo in particular. A racy Sauvignon Blanc from New Zealand or the Cape will fill in splendidly.

An interesting question, one which throws up a side of wine much neglected (even by food and wine writers, who might be expected to know better), is this: does the nature of this dish, being both gelid and jellied, matter in the choice of wine? The answer is yes, very much so. If this soup were warm, the Manzanilla would not work as effectively as it does. The reason is the texture of the solid soup and its temperature. The Manzanilla, as a result of its own texture as a liquid, seems utterly to meld with it. If, however, the dish's ingredients were warmed – just warmed, not even cooked through – this wine would not be as companionable as a Forrest Estate Sauvignon Blanc (from New Zealand) or Neil Ellis Groenekloof Sauvignon Blanc (from South Africa). Texture, it seems to me, is as important as, sometimes more so than, the fruit or fruits one finds in a wine when one is deciding how it will work with a dish.

WINE CHECKLIST

MANZANILLA (SPAIN)

SAUVIGNON BLANC (NEW ZEALAND AND SOUTH AFRICA)

WINE AND PEPPERS

One could write a book on this seemingly naive subject. Let me make some broad observations. First, hot peppers. With meat and/or vegetable dishes, these require a wine with a characteristic edge which can be defined as fruitily sweet. Zinfandel, Pinotage, Shiraz from the New World work well. With fish or shellfish dishes with hot peppers, these wines often work just as effectively. However, with mussels, squid, and prawn dishes, a white wine is perhaps better, one with the bite of that Kiwi Sauvignon Blanc. Bell peppers, raw in salads, go best with Rieslings. When peppers are cooked in a stew, there are other ingredients which will take precedence, but in general I would veer toward reds with soft fruit but a degree of tannin to give them depth: Rhônes, Syrahs, Shirazes from McLaren Vale, and wines from Bordeaux.

Carrot and Cumin Salad

SERVES 4 AS A SALAD

I HAVE A THING ABOUT CUMIN; it's one of the many spices found in curries that gives that addictiveness and craving for more. In North Africa, cumin is used a lot as it is in this simple dish with just carrots. We don't do anything as interesting with carrots, do we? The sweetness of the carrots and the warming flavour of the cumin are just perfect for each other.

1 ONION, FINELY CHOPPED | 4TBSP OLIVE OIL | 1TSP GROUND CUMIN | 1TSP CUMIN SEEDS | 6 MEDIUM-SIZED CARROTS, PEELED AND THINLY SLICED | 100ML (3½FL OZ) ORANGE JUICE | SALT AND FRESHLY GROUND BLACK PEPPER | 1TBSP CHOPPED CORIANDER

1. Gently cook the onion in the olive oil with the ground cumin and seeds on a low heat for 4–5 minutes, without colouring. Stir every so often.

2. Add the carrots and pour in the orange juice. Season and add enough water just to cover the carrots. Bring to the boil, cover with a lid, and simmer until just tender.

3. Turn the heat up and cook on a medium heat, uncovered, until almost all the liquid has evaporated. Leave to cool. Stir in the coriander and serve the carrots at room temperature.

MEDITERRANEAN SALADS

All over the Mediterranean you will come across decent salads that are put together with style and very simple ingredients. When you have good produce, there is little need to do too much to it other than add a couple of other good-quality ingredients and some olive oil. My local Turkish restaurant, the Mangal Ockabashi, serves the most amazing tomato salad: finely chopped tomatoes and onion, then just simply bound in a little olive oil with coriander and a sprinkling of sumac (a dried crushed berry used in Mediterranean and Middle Eastern cooking). It also makes a great aubergine salad where the aubergine gets thrown into the charcoal until it's blackened, then is just scooped out and mixed with crushed garlic, olive oil, and peppers that have also been roasted over the charcoal. I would always advocate cooking with specific ingredients in mind as opposed to throwing them together in the hope of creating a dish. The simpler, the better.

CARROT AND CUMIN SALAD

NOW, I APPRECIATE THAT THIS DISH IS NOT GOING TO BE EATEN BY ITSELF but may well accompany some grilled sausages or lamb cutlets. It could even sit alongside (or even underneath on the same plate) some pan-fried fish fillets such as salmon. In either case, I want to see red wine served here, and a degree of daintiness is to be desired in this liquid. Otherwise, the sweetness of the carrots will overwhelm it. It is, therefore, a good idea to chill a bottle of Villa Maria Pinot Noir, or a Californian, or, and this is a rare intrusion, one from Burgundy. A ten-year-old Domaine Leroy Pommard would be splendid if you could find one (I have three bottles left and they're not for sale for all the money in the world), and so would anything by Réné Engel where the degree of nice spice he gets in his Pinots would be excellent to offset the cumin seeds. But, equally as well as a red, certain whites work with this dish, and one is Flagstone Two Roads Chardonnay in the screwcap from the Cape.

WINE CHECKLIST

PINOT NOIR (NEW ZEALAND, CALIFORNIA – THE USA, AND BURGUNDY – FRANCE)

CHARDONNAY (SOUTH AFRICA)

WINE AND MEDITERRANEAN SALADS

Sumac is as subtle or as pervasive as lime juice can be. It depends on the amount you use. In the tomato salad specified I would drink Rieslings (from the usual suspects). Mediterranean salads, in general, enjoy being partnered by such white wines, though if the said salads are French or Italian in origin I would also press the case for the inclusion of Pinot Grigio, from northern Italy, and Picpoul de Pinet, from southern France, on the wine list. With the Turkish aubergine salad Mark mentions, I would go for red wine. Any of the reds specified on this page would be tantalizingly perfect. Another so-called salad is, of course, hummous. I find it goes rather well with Retsina. This unjustly neglected wine, of Greece and Cyprus, is excellent, also, with many Mediterranean-style salads.

Butternut Squash and Ginger Soup

SERVES 4–6

SQUASHES AND PUMPKINS RARELY GET USED AT HOME TO THEIR FULL POTENTIAL, except perhaps at Hallowe'en. They come in all different shapes, colours, and sizes, and some have more worthwhile culinary qualities than others. My favourite is the butternut squash; it's always sweet and has a deep, vibrant colour with a better ratio of flesh to skin than some of the larger varieties.

1 SMALL LEEK, ROUGHLY CHOPPED | 1 SMALL ONION, ROUGHLY CHOPPED | 30G (1OZ) ROOT GINGER, PEELED AND FINELY CHOPPED OR GRATED | GOOD KNOB OF BUTTER | 1KG (2LB 4OZ) BUTTERNUT SQUASH, PEELED, SEEDED, AND ROUGHLY CHOPPED | ½ LITRE (18FL OZ) VEGETABLE STOCK (A GOOD-QUALITY CUBE WILL DO) | SALT AND FRESHLY GROUND BLACK PEPPER | 1TBSP PUMPKIN SEEDS, LIGHTLY TOASTED

1. Gently cook the leek, onion, and ginger in the butter until softened. Add the butternut squash and stock, bring to the boil, season with salt and pepper, then simmer for 20 minutes.

2. Blend the soup in a liquidizer until smooth, then strain through a fine-meshed sieve. Reheat the soup, and adjust the consistency with a little vegetable stock or water if necessary.

3. Check the seasoning and serve straight away with a sprinkling of the toasted pumpkin seeds.

GINGER

The taste of ginger is quite sensational, and the intensity and aroma just feel as if they're doing you good. Apart from being heavily used in Asian cooking, it finds its way into Italian and Spanish dishes, probably from the North African influence just across the water. I always like to keep a piece of root ginger in my refrigerator at home, because you never know when it's going to come in handy. Apart from being tossed around in a wok, ginger makes great drinks. Fresh ginger beer is refreshing, and ginger makes great tea just grated and infused in hot water along with a spoonful of honey.

BUTTERNUT SQUASH AND GINGER SOUP

TO WORK OUT THE WINE TO GO WITH THIS DISH, IT IS NECESSARY TO WATCH THE FAMOUS ASCOT RACES ON TV. These take place in June every year and are broadcast around the world. One of the features, for many of us the truly significant feature, is the hats the ladies wear. Those toppings dictate all that takes place underneath, from the dress and jewellery right through to the shoes. Mysteriously, though, they dictate far more. They seem to stimulate the horses and jockeys themselves, and often you will find, in the winners' enclosure, the trappings of the jockeys matching those of the hats closest to each horse. In other words, a good deal of sympathetic collusion has gone on, and it is the same with the toppings in this dish. Ginger, whether ground or fresh, determines the style of the wine, and my hand unhesitatingly hovers over Verdelho from Moondah Brook in Western Australia and New Zealand's Montana Church Road Chardonnay Chardonnay. Certain Pinot Blancs from Alsace are also in the frame.

WINE CHECKLIST

VERDELHO (WESTERN AUSTRALIA)

CHARDONNAY (HAWKE'S BAY – NEW ZEALAND)

PINOT BLANC (ALSACE – FRANCE)

WINE AND GINGER

Mark makes out a great case for keeping a piece of fresh stem ginger in the fridge and I would add further to his enthusiasm. How do you feel about spritzers? I find that the cheapest German white wine, one with a definite sweet undertone, is great as the basis of a summer – a torrid summer – pick-me-up aperitif, and as a general refresher, added to sparkling mineral water.

The ginger can either be added as a small coin-sized lump or, better, grated and packed in a small muslin sheet and left to float in the drink (this way you get more gingery release and no shreds getting in the teeth). Ginger as an ingredient is only a small part of a dish, but it is mightily, deliciously, pervasive. With a chicken stew, the wine required is a light, tangy red – something you can chill like a white wine. For fish dishes with ginger I would look at German Rieslings, Kiwi Sauvignon Blancs, Alsatian Pinot Blancs and Gewurztraminers, and Aussie Semillons. The odd thing about ginger is that though it is pervasive it is not at odds with other ingredients.

This is particularly true of its inclusion in Indian, Pakistani, and Bangladeshi dishes, where it heightens the effect of chillies, coriander, cardamom, turmeric, and so on. In these instances, I invariably reach for an Australian Shiraz.

Boiled Duck's Eggs with Asparagus Soldiers

SERVES 4

THIS DISH IS CATCHING ON, AND I'VE EVEN SEEN IT ON THE MENU IN SOHO HOUSE, New York. It's simple and fun, and there seems to be no problems getting your hands on duck's eggs these days. If you are making these at home for a large gathering, you may want to try to get your hands on one of those egg topper gadgets. I bought one ages ago and haven't used it yet, but my kitchen drawers are full of those things that I think are good ideas at the time. If you can't get your hands on duck's eggs, then buy extra large hen's eggs.

4 DUCK'S EGGS | 1KG (2LB 4OZ) MEDIUM THICKNESS ASPARAGUS, WOODY STEMS REMOVED | MALDON SEA SALT | CELERY SALT

1. Have two pots of water boiling: one salted for the asparagus, and one for the eggs. Using a slotted spoon, carefully place the eggs into the pan of unsalted water. Set a timer for 6 minutes for duck's eggs and a minute or so less for hen's. Transfer the eggs onto a plate and put the asparagus into the boiling salted water for 5 minutes.

2. Using a small knife (or you can use a special egg topper), carefully remove the tops from the eggs, then replace them to keep them hot. Put them into egg cups on warm plates.

3. Check the asparagus by piercing through a thick end. When tender, drain in a colander, then arrange in bundles next to the eggs. Spoon a little pile of Maldon sea salt and celery salt onto each plate and serve.

HOLLANDAISE SAUCE

Asparagus just wouldn't be the same without this thick, rich, buttery, and delicious sauce. If, at any time, the sauce should separate on you, put a teaspoonful of boiling water in a clean bowl and very slowly whisk the separated sauce into that – it should come together again magically in front of your eyes.

Serves 4–6 Put 3tbsp white wine vinegar, 1 chopped small shallot, a few sprigs of tarragon, 1 bay leaf, and 5 black peppercorns in a pan with 3tbsp water. Boil for a few minutes to reduce the liquid to about a dessertspoonful. Strain, then leave to cool.

Melt 200g (7oz) unsalted butter in a small pan and allow to simmer for 5 minutes. Leave to cool a little, then pour off the pure butter where it has separated from the whey. Discard the whey. Using this clarified butter helps to keep the sauce thick and discourage separation. Put 3 small egg yolks in a small bowl (or double boiler if you have one) with half the vinegar reduction and whisk over a pan of gently simmering water until it begins to thicken and become frothy.

Slowly trickle in the butter, whisking continuously (an electric hand whisk will help). If the butter is added too quickly, the sauce will separate.

When you have added two-thirds of the butter, taste the sauce and add a little more, or all, of the remaining vinegar reduction. Add the rest of the butter. The sauce should not be too vinegary, but the vinegar should just cut the oiliness of the butter.

Season the sauce with salt and white pepper, cover with clingfilm, and leave in a warm, not hot, place until needed. It can be reheated over a bowl of hot water and lightly whisked again. Either spoon it over the tips of the cooked asparagus, or serve separately in small bowls.

BOILED DUCK'S EGGS WITH ASPARAGUS SOLDIERS

A MAN WHO MAKES HIS OWN CELERY SALT IS TO BE WORSHIPPED. A woman who makes her own celery salt is to be wooed. In both instances, a degree of fear is involved, but as far as the wine waiter is concerned there is an added delicacy: choosing the wrong wine when an ingredient like that makes so distinctive a contribution to the dish could be a disaster. For celery salt enhances the intensity of the asparagus which, unadorned, basks in the glory of an already legendary reputation for being difficult to pair with wine.

My solution is to avoid Sauvignon Blancs, which are the plodder's choice, and go for Rieslings without too much sweetness. Therefore, Kabinetts from the Rheingau (Weingut Bathalsar Ress Kabinett) and the Mosel (Weingut Reichsgraf Von Kesselstatt), and dryish Rieslings from the Clare Valley (Grosset Polish Hill Riesling and Mount Horrocks Watervale Riesling), are the order of the day. And if we can find any with sufficient bottle-age, so that there has been bequeathed to them that undertone of petroleum (often likened to Plasticine or kerosene), then so much the better. This does not sound a charming personality trait to discover in any wine, but, believe me, with this dish it is wonderfully apt.

Such Rieslings, high in tartaric rather than malic acid (because they have not undergone the secondary or malolactic fermentation which reds and many whites such as Chardonnay undergo), become oily and highly aromatic with age, and even at twenty years old, in screwcap, such a wine is glorious alongside asparagus with celery salt. Asparagus is tricky because it contains asparagine which is crystallized nitrogen. This has an after-effect on the digestive system, of course. It is added evidence of the difficulties the vegetable poses when selecting the right bottle.

WINE CHECKLIST

RIESLING KABINETT (RHEINGAU AND MOSEL – GERMANY)

RIESLING (CLARE VALLEY – SOUTH AUSTRALIA)

WINE AND EGG-BASED SAUCES

The only eggs which do dictate the style of wine are fish eggs (from caviar to taramasalata), and so it is very much the additions to the eggs in any sauce which influence vinous decisions. The hollandaise sauce with asparagus has shallots, tarragon, and, most important of all, the vinegar, and this makes the wines above, which take celery salt into account, slightly less effective.

With hollandaise sauce, then, with our asparagus I'm plumping for slightly fruitier styles: unwooded Chardonnays from Australia, young demi-sec Vouvrays from the Loire, Tokay Pinot Gris from Alsace, and Chardonnays from Chile and Argentina.

But what of other egg-based sauces, such as Béarnaise? The wine choices here cannot solely be matched to the sauce alone, ignoring the dish's main ingredient over which it will be poured, but in the case of Béarnaise, which also features vinegar, I would, if the main ingredient was fish, go for the wines just mentioned; if the main ingredient were meat, such as chicken breast, I would prefer reds. The grape would be Cabernet Franc, the wine would be a Loire Chinon or Bourgueil.

Catalan Broad Beans with Chorizo

SERVES 4

I HAD A DISH VERY SIMILAR TO THIS ON THE COSTA BRAVA, and, in its simplicity, it struck me as being a classic summertime dish. In the winter, frozen beans would work perfectly well in this instance. Broad beans can be a little dull, but the piquant chorizo really brings them to life. You need to buy the cooking chorizo, *parilla*, for this dish, as it is a lot softer in texture and less harsh when cooked. You can even buy little cocktail chorizo that make perfect tapas.

1 SMALL ONION, FINELY CHOPPED | 2 CLOVES GARLIC, CRUSHED | 60ML (2¼FL OZ) EXTRA-VIRGIN OLIVE OIL | 100G (3½OZ) SMALL COOKING CHORIZO, SLICED, OR LEFT WHOLE FOR THE COCKTAIL SIZE | 1TSP TOMATO PUREE | 200ML (7FL OZ) CHICKEN STOCK | SALT AND FRESHLY GROUND BLACK PEPPER | 500G (1LB 2OZ) BROAD BEANS (SHELLED WEIGHT)

1. Gently cook the onion and garlic in the olive oil until soft. Add the chorizo, tomato purée and chicken stock. Bring to the boil, season with salt and pepper, and simmer gently for 15 minutes.

2. Meanwhile cook the broad beans for 5 minutes in boiling salted water (allow 2–3 minutes if cooking from frozen), add them to the chorizo, and continue to simmer for a further 15 minutes.

3. If the liquid has evaporated, add a little more chicken stock or water. The beans and chorizo should be just bound in the liquid that's left. Season again with salt and pepper if necessary.

BEANS

Pods are a great thing, and it's a shame that beans such as borlotti, cannellini, chick peas, and flageolets aren't as readily available in their fresh form as they are abroad. We tend to see them as canned or dried specimens, but these can be disappointing. The canned ones have more often than not been cooked a bit too much, and the dried ones, having been dried for too long, don't reconstitute to satisfaction.

There are, however, some excellent dried Spanish beans around, and it's worth paying more for the quality. Always remember to soak dried beans in plenty of water and top up if necessary. When it comes to cooking, a little bicarbonate of soda helps to soften them.

With today's demand for imported produce, specialist delis and greengrocers are now stocking pods such as borlotti which have the most amazing streaks of red colouring, both on the pod and on the bean. Unfortunately, the stripes disappear when you cook the beans, but they are delicious just cooked in water, olive oil, rosemary, and garlic with perhaps some diced pancetta.

CATALAN BROAD BEANS WITH CHORIZO

CHORIZO IS A DECISIVE INGREDIENT HERE. It has texture and flavour which together give an oily, ripely spicy overtone to the beans, and this is why a red wine, which may seem preferable to some palates, has to be chosen with care. However, I prefer a white wine here, but its fruit must not be too delicate. Viognier, for instance, is too suave for this dish. Even one of those wonderfully robust Viogniers from Yalumba in Australia will not stand up. Tokay Pinot Gris is better, even a Gewurztraminer from Chile (try Concha y Toro – not so heady as the Alsatian specimens), and some of the woody Chardonnays, which I usually detest as glugging bottles.

Another good choice here is a South African Chenin Blanc, especially one which is not too young so it has a mature, more vegetal undertone to its essential crispness, such as Villiera. Why white wines like this? Because broad beans are the richest beans there are, it seems to me (haricot beans come closest), and chorizo is a very brash sausage. The combination, delightfully uplifting though it is, does need a wine which cuts through the unabashed richness of the dish and both refreshes the palate and enhances the experience of the beans and sausage. The dish performs similarly with the wine, enhancing the fruit, hence that Chilean Gewurztraminer in the photograph. I recall Mark's assistant chef – helping to prepare the dishes under Mark's supervision for Jason Lowe, the photographer – being bowled over by taking a mouthful of the wine with the dish. It is an impressive pairing, and as Jason said when he finished clicking away and got stuck into both: "Stone the crows, Malcolm, isn't this the business, eh?"

WINE CHECKLIST

TOKAY PINOT GRIS (ALSACE – FRANCE)

GEWURZTRAMINER (CHILE)

CHENIN BLANC (SOUTH AFRICA)

Roasted Jerusalem Artichokes with Bacon and Rosemary

SERVES 4 AS A STARTER OR 6 AS A SIDE DISH

IT'S A SHAME THE POOR OLD JERUSALEM ARTICHOKE DOESN'T LOOK AS ATTRACTIVE AS SOME OF ITS TUBEROUS RELATIVES. I reckon its flavour has got a lot going for it if only shoppers would take the leap and add this knobbly brown root to their shopping basket. Restaurants are doing their bit, though, to encourage diners by matching Jerusalem artichokes with scallops and all sorts of other delights, because they are so versatile.

4TBSP OLIVE OIL | 1KG (2LB 4OZ) JERUSALEM ARTICHOKES, PEELED AND HALVED IF LARGE | SALT AND FRESHLY GROUND BLACK PEPPER | 1 ONION, CHOPPED | 6 RASHERS THICK, RINDLESS STREAKY BACON OR PANCETTA, CUT INTO ROUGH 2CM CUBES | A FEW SPRIGS OF ROSEMARY, LEAVES REMOVED AND ROUGHLY CHOPPED | GOOD KNOB OF BUTTER

1. Preheat the oven to 200°C/400°F/ Gas mark 6. Heat a roasting tray in the oven with 3 tbsp of the olive oil for about 5 minutes. Add the Jerusalem artichokes, season and roast for 30 minutes, stirring every so often.

2. Meanwhile cook the onion in the remaining olive oil with the bacon or pancetta for 4–5 minutes on a low heat without colouring, stirring now and again.

3. Add the onion mixture to the roasting tray with the Jerusalem artichokes, and stir in the rosemary. Roast for another 20 minutes, stirring occasionally, until golden. If they are browning too much, turn the oven down or cover with foil. Stir in a knob of butter and serve.

AROMATIC HERBS

We are becoming more and more confident about using fresh herbs. They are always readily available and well displayed in supermarkets and greengrocers. If you have a garden, then I strongly recommend you grow as many different herbs, and salad leaves for that matter, as possible and experiment with different ones.

You can't beat just going to the garden for a handful of fresh herbs for cooking or to use in salads. Herbs such as chervil, flat parsley, and chives make a delicious summery salad with some home-grown leaves such as land cress, rocket, or even those mixtures that grow back again once they have been cut.

ROASTED JERUSALEM ARTICHOKES WITH BACON AND ROSEMARY

SHIRAZ MAKES A MARVELLOUS COMPANION FOR THIS DISH. Examples from Western Australia (Cape Mentelle with three or four years of bottle-age, so that there is an undertone of burned licorice, is perfect) jostle for premier position with those from McLaren Vale in South Australia, where I would especially single out the one from Coriole Vineyards, shown in the photograph. Fairview Estate blends from the Cape are also good, as well as certain Zinfandels from California. Of course, this dish will acompany some others, but to avoid overpowering the artichokes, and to find a wine that will instead work with them, then my wine choices are just the ticket.

WINE CHECKLIST

SHIRAZ (WESTERN AUSTRALIA, AND McLAREN VALE – SOUTH AUSTRALIA)

SHIRAZ BLENDS (SOUTH AFRICA)

ZINFANDEL (CALIFORNIA – THE USA)

WINE AND AROMATIC HERBS

Only where the most resonant herbs are concerned does the wine choice need to reflect their presence. These herbs are tarragon, curry leaf, sage, basil, mint, and thyme. Tarragon is wonderfully versatile.

With fish, any of the Rieslings I've chosen in this book are sensible choices. For tarragon with gherkins or cucumbers, Retsina from Greece. With chicken, you go either white or red: an Aussie Chardonnay or a Cabernet Franc from the Loire. Curry leaf tends to be with other spices, and Aussie Shiraz might well be the wine to choose. Sage is usually with meat, and big reds are required, such as Barolo, and Cabernets from Coonawarra in Australia. Basil tends to feature automatically with tomatoes, and so anything I have so far written about tomatoes applies here. Mint is most interesting as it allows Muscats, highly perfumed wines, to come into the picture. Thyme is usually with other herbs, though when it is used alone, I like rosé wines.

Gobi Bhaji

SERVES 4-6

I'M NOT SURE WHETHER MANY PEOPLE ORDER THIS DISH, but it certainly seems to appear on most Indian restaurant menus. The subtle spices and herbs add to the sweetness of the cauliflower when it goes beyond *al dente* stage. Give it a try next time you visit your local Indian restaurant.

3TBSP **GHEE OR VEGETABLE OIL** | 20G (¾OZ) **ROOT GINGER, PEELED AND FINELY GRATED OR CHOPPED** | 1 **SMALL MEDIUM-HEAT GREEN CHILLI, SEEDED AND FINELY CHOPPED** | **GOOD PINCH OF CURRY LEAVES** | 1TSP **MUSTARD SEEDS** | ½TSP **GROUND TURMERIC OR** 1TSP **FRESH, PEELED, AND FINELY GRATED** | 1TSP **GROUND CUMIN** | ½TSP **CUMIN SEEDS** | 1TSP **GROUND CORIANDER** | 1TSP **GARAM MASALA** | 1 **MEDIUM HEAD OF CAULIFLOWER, CUT INTO EVEN-SIZED FLORETS (LARGE ONES HALVED)** | **JUICE OF HALF A LEMON** | 500ML(18FL OZ) **VEGETABLE STOCK** | **SALT** | 2TBSP **CHOPPED FRESH CORIANDER**

1. Heat the ghee in a heavy-bottomed saucepan and add the ginger, chilli, curry leaves, mustard seeds, and spices. Gently cook on a low heat for 2–3 minutes.

2. Add the cauliflower, lemon juice, and vegetable stock, season with a good pinch of salt and bring to the boil. Stir well, cover and cook on a very low heat, stirring every so often, for 15 minutes, or until they are just cooked.

3. Remove the lid and cook on a slightly higher heat until almost all the liquid has evaporated. Drain what is left into a pan and boil until there is enough just to coat the cauliflower. Stir it and the coriander back into the pan.

INDIAN SPICES

My cupboard at home is full of spices – mainly Indian ones. I'm lucky that I have Brick Lane on my doorstep; the range of spices in small and large quantities is just too tempting. A bit of advice though: don't be tempted to buy bulk spices because they look a bargain. They lose their aromas once they are stored for too long, so buy smaller amounts more frequently.

The secret of good Indian food is to be able to taste the different spice flavours. I like to taste a cardamom pod occasionally or to pick out a hint of cinnamon. Using different spices instead of just throwing in a bit of curry powder makes a lot of difference. Certain spices are good with fish, some are better with meat, and others with vegetables. Some curries benefit from having the spices roasted beforehand to give the sauce a dark and nutty taste.

Curries are not always hot and spicy; a curry is simply a highly spiced dish with a wonderful aromatic quality. Try adding curry and methi leaves to dishes, along with a handful of fresh coriander leaves at the end for fragrance.

GOBI BHAJI

TO GO WITH WHAT EXACTLY? AH, THAT IS THE QUESTION! Whether 'tis nobler to take this dish as it is or to enjoy it with some roasted meat or a lemon-juice-marinated, herb-grilled escalope of chicken. I have to admit that this diversity of choice does not make my job any easier or even possible, but I shall press ahead on the assumption that this gobi bhaji dominates the plate and thus we select, with nary a tremble of the wrist, Aussie Shiraz. What has made this wine so adored by drinkers the world over is its sweetness without soppiness, richness without clottedness, quaffability without mono-dimensionality. It is precisely those strengths that make it so good with spiced dishes such as this. Amen. End of sermon.

Or, rather, let me take this opportunity to commence on an extension of the same sermon. Now, Shiraz candidates for the gobi bhaji are dotted throughout this book, but some of these are not cheap. So let me point out that you do not have to spend a lot of money to get the right Shiraz for this dish (or many another Indian, Pakistani or Bangladeshi dish, particularly if they have a lot of spices lurking in their fabric ready to inflame the palate). The reason is that chilli, coriander, cardamom, turmeric, garam masala, fenugreek, and all those other microscopic, but sometimes lethal, additions to such cuisines blend harmoniously with a red wine with an emphatically fruity presence.

Most mainstream European red wines do not take to the cooking of the Indian sub-continent, but Shiraz is perfectly at home. Syrah, on the other hand, though it is the same grape variety, does not necessarily perform in the same way. With a really virile curry, an inexpensive Aussie Shiraz – not a lot of complexity, few tannins, a touch of undertonal sweetness – accommodates itself to the food wonderfully.

Can I persuade people that beer is a lousy accompaniment on such occasions? Only when they experience the brilliance of the marriage, and the superb sum of its parts, and recognize that red wine is both a cooling and an enhancing presence (which beer cannot be, as it merely wipes the palate clean), do they come to appreciate that here is one of the most sublime of food and wine couplings.

In some cases, white wine serves the purpose of this sublime marriage. A dish of masala dosai, for example, stuffed with piquant mashed potato and with a gorgeously chewy coconut chutney on the side, is superb with a German Riesling of Spätlese ripeness. And that really is the end of the sermon.

Tagliolini with Wild Mushrooms

SERVES 4

I HAVE A SLIGHT OBSESSION WITH FUNGI. I will go and pick my own at the drop of a hat, given the opportunity. I'm not suggesting you all go mushroom-picking to create this dish, as you need a bit of know-how and a good nose, rather like Malcolm. If you are going to make mushroom pasta, I highly recommend you use fresh mushrooms in season and definitely not the dried sort. There are lots of cultivated varieties around now which would make a good alternative to the real wild ones. Porcini powder is dried, ground-up porcini mushrooms with the consistency of flour. It gives a little more depth to the sauce, instead of going to the trouble of making mushroom stock. You can get it in good Italian delis or special sections in supermarkets.

1TBSP OLIVE OIL | **250G (9OZ) SEASONAL WILD MUSHROOMS, CLEANED** | **3 CLOVES GARLIC, CRUSHED** | **250G (9OZ) MASCARPONE** | **½TSP PORCINI POWDER (OPTIONAL)** | **2TBSP CHOPPED PARSLEY** | **SALT AND FRESHLY GROUND BLACK PEPPER** | **80G (2¾OZ) TAGLIOLINI**

1. Take a large, nonstick frying pan and heat it with the olive oil until almost smoking. Sauté the mushrooms with the garlic in a couple of batches until they begin to colour. Remove from the heat and transfer to a plate. Leave to one side while you make the sauce.

2. Return the pan to the heat, add the mascarpone and porcini powder and heat gently until the mascarpone has melted. Simmer on a low heat until it thickens, then add the mushrooms along with any juices. Stir in the parsley, and season.

3. Bring back to the boil and simmer for another minute or so until the sauce thickens – the juices will have thinned the mascarpone. Meanwhile, cook the pasta in boiling salted water, according to the packet instructions. Drain in a colander. Mix the sauce with the pasta and season if necessary.

PASTA

Ever get confused which pasta to buy? I am convinced that pasta companies just sit around a big table and constantly come up with new, mad names for their products. I mean, "radiatore", where did that come from and what would you use that for, I wonder? I've seen ones in gift shops that represent sexual organs. You couldn't serve them, could you?

Dried or fresh? Good question. Purist Italians will often go for good-quality dried across the board, even if they make it themselves and dry it afterward. Fresh pasta, though, is good for some dishes with gutsy meaty sauces such as hare ragú or duck sauce, whereas a fresh tomato sauce is more suited to a fine dried pasta. It's a big topic, and I'm sure Italians argue among themselves over which is correct: fresh, egg-based, semolina, etc.

I think it becomes a personal preference at the end of the day, and getting the sauce right is as important as choosing the right type of pasta.

TAGLIOLINI WITH WILD MUSHROOMS

AH! I SMELL PINOT NOIR! DON'T YOU? But not Burgundian Pinot Noir. Oh, dear me, no. We must repair to New Zealand, California, South Africa, Australia, and Chile, my dears. Indeed, Chilean Pinot is getting so good that I suspect it is threatening to borrow a phrase once applied to sherry: *Solo hay dos clases de Pinot de Chile, el bueno y el mejor* (there are only two kinds of Chilean Pinot Noir, the good and the best).

I have been particularly taken with Cono Sur and Montes, but for this dish, with those gamy mushrooms, you might try to find Leyda Valley Pinot Noir from the Leyda Estate. The last vintages I tried each offered a compelling aroma of burned, savoury cherries, and there were tannins of eyebrow-raising length and cohesion (though not craggy depth). It is never wise to offer blanket approval of a wine, a grape variety, a region, a vintage, or a country. But for Chilean Pinot Noir, I rack my brains – what there is left of them after four decades of dedicated vinous study and applied research – and I find I cannot think of a single Chilean Pinot, of vintages since 1999, that I did not like. Of course, there were eccentrics, some bizarre curiousities, and I am aware that some of my peers in the world of wine tasting do not find Chilean Pinot as congenial as I. But these fellows are, I find, all young men (not women), and thus they have not, like me, experienced the burgundies of the late 1950s and the 1960s, of which these Chileans remind me. So, is it all sentimentality on my part? Maybe.

WINE CHECKLIST

PINOT NOIR (NEW ZEALAND, CALIFORNIA – THE USA, SOUTH AFRICA, AUSTRALIA, AND CHILE)

WINE AND PASTA

I chose Pinot Noir to go with the tagliolini dish on account of the mushrooms. They wholly dictated the style of the accompanying wine. I do not know of any pasta except black squid-ink linguine which would decisively influence my choice of wine. With the latter pasta, because it almost exclusively (certainly in my house, at least) goes with a squid or prawn sauce of some kind, I invariably choose a crisp white wine such as Loire Savennières made from the Chenin Blanc grape.

If there is chilli in the dish, then I prefer fuller whites such as an Aussie Semillon (one with five or six years of bottle-age under its belt). But other pastas and noodles? Difficult to be so specific. It all depends on what the sauce is – unless the dish is Thai, in which case I like NZ Sauvignon Blanc. Pasta in the form of oriental wontons, with either fish or meat fillings, invariably has me reaching for an Alsatian or a German wine – a Tokay Pinot Gris or a Riesling Spätlese.

Risotto with Périgord Truffles

SERVES 4

WHY THE HELL IS HE GIVING US A RECIPE FOR TRUFFLES? You can't buy the things anywhere, except in jars. True, but this is also a reference book that you may find handy when you are confronted with them on a restaurant menu or in a specialist shop. Black truffles which come mainly from the Périgord region of France, or Norcia in Italy, are about a third of the price of their cousins, the white truffle. If you are a truffle fan, you will probably own a truffle shaver which is a dinky, little slicing contraption with a sharp, adjustable blade for slicing these little gems. The black truffle season starts in about December, depending on the weather, and runs through 'till about March. Don't be tempted by the cheaper summer truffles as they are white inside and have very little aroma.

70G (2½OZ) BUTTER | 200G (7OZ) CARNAROLI RICE | MUSHROOM STOCK | SALT AND FRESHLY GROUND WHITE PEPPER | 1TBSP DOUBLE CREAM | 40G (1½OZ) PERIGORD TRUFFLE, LIGHTLY BRUSHED IF DIRTY
FOR THE MUSHROOM STOCK
1 SMALL ONION, ROUGHLY CHOPPED | HALF A LEEK, ROUGHLY CHOPPED | 2 CLOVES GARLIC, ROUGHLY CHOPPED | 1TBSP VEGETABLE OIL | 150G (5½OZ) BUTTON MUSHROOMS, ROUGHLY CHOPPED | 10G (¼OZ) DRIED CEPS, SOAKED FOR 2 HOURS IN A LITTLE WARM WATER AND DRAINED | 5 BLACK PEPPERCORNS

1. First, make the stock. Gently cook the onion, leek, and garlic in the oil without colouring until soft. Add the rest of the ingredients and cover with about 1½ litres of water. Bring to the boil and simmer gently for 1 hour, skimming occasionally. Strain through a fine-meshed sieve, and keep hot if using straight away. The stock should be strongly flavoured; if not, reduce it for a more concentrated flavour.

2. To make the risotto, take a heavy-bottomed pan and melt 30g of the butter. Add the rice and stir for a minute on a low heat with a wooden spoon. Gradually add the stock a little at a time, stirring constantly and ensuring that each addition of liquid has been fully absorbed by the rice before adding the next. Season with salt and freshly ground black pepper.

3. When the rice is almost cooked, stir in the remaining butter along with the cream. Check the seasoning, and correct if necessary. The risotto should be moist but not stodgy. Spoon the risotto onto plates or into pasta bowls and shave the truffles generously over each one. Serve immediately.

RICE DISHES

It's crucial to select the correct rice for your dish – something you don't have to be so strict with when it comes to pasta. I've seen basmati rice being used on menus for risotto, which is just crazy and missing the point completely. For risotto, you need a rice whose grains will stay intact but will allow the flavours of the stock to be absorbed. This is why carnaroli, arborio, and vialone nano are best.

The preparation of paella needs a type such as Valencia, a similarly robust but less starch-releasing rice than the risotto type. A rice pudding uses a rice which will release starch and not disintegrate. Basmati, unlike the others, requires simple and delicate cooking so that the end result is fragrant, light, and fluffy. Luckily, shops and supermarkets are stocking most types of rice these days.

RISOTTO WITH PERIGORD TRUFFLES

PINOTAGE, THE HOME-GROWN CAPE GRAPE, is an interesting choice here, but perhaps a controversial one. Is it too rubbery? Too brash? Several of the more compelling Pinotages have already been mentioned in this book – Clos Malverne, Kanonkop, and Spice Route – but I'd like to add some further thoughts on this grape and also to extend the repertoire of wines to drink with this dish. Now, why I like Pinotage in the first place with truffles, when they are the flavour-controller in a risotto, is not only because of the taste, but equally because of the texture. There is something so unctuous, sumptuous, and sybaritic about a risotto (the ultimate comfort food in many respects) that its suavity, which the prickly gentility of the quasi-*al dente* nature of the rice only marginally mollifies, requires its wine to display a contrary personality. Hence, Pinotage – the bravura examples of which offer a chewiness and thickness of texture which is most appealing with the rice and those truffles (themselves ever so slightly crunchy).

But what of other wines? Perfume is important (which Pinotage, with its spiced cherry or plum overtone and charred undertone, offers), but certain other wines perform well here. One above all is Cabernet Franc, that unsung Bordeaux constituent, which for some years now has featured with distinction in the lists of the more interesting wines grown in Australia, California, Argentina, Washington State, New Zealand, and a few other places.

However, it is in its exclusively Anjou-Touraine manifestation in the Loire, where it is not in cahoots with any other grape variety or varieties but a superb solo performer, that I wish to commend to you its peculiar affinity with this dish. The area names are myriad: Bourgueil, Chinon, and Saumur-Champigny are my favourites, but Coteaux du Loir, Fiefs Vendéens, Thouarsais, Coteaux d'Ancenis, Touraine-Mesland are a few others, and the list goes on. What Bourgueil, Chinon, and Saumur-Champigny display so grittily is both a chewiness (like coal in some instances) and a magnificent overtone of mineral slatiness. This is a tannic phenomenon, and it is wonderful with truffle risotto (best is a wine of three to seven years of age or, in some instances, much older).

Individual names to single out are Caslot-Galbrun, Filliatreau, Chasle, Denis Duveau, Couly-Dutheil, Druet, Charles Joguet, Gérard Spelty, Clos des Cordeliers, and Edouard Pisani-Ferry (Château de Targé). With other rice dishes of a savoury nature, such as paella, the wines above are perfect (even if the paella contains seafood).

WINE CHECKLIST

PINOTAGE (SOUTH AFRICA)

CABERNET FRANC (LOIRE – FRANCE)

2
Fish and Shellfish

AS A KID, I LOVED THE SEA AND EVERYTHING TO DO WITH IT. Well, you would, I suppose, if sea gulls woke you every morning, and the sound of waves crashing on the beach replaced the buzz of the alarm clock. I fished as a kid in between playing golf and going to school, and why the hell wouldn't you if you were brought up in such an amazing part of the country as Dorset? I would catch mackerel by the bagful, and other fish such as pollack, if I was lucky enough to get out on a boat. It was a natural way of life, even if it did kill my pleasure time. Unfortunately, these days, as consumers, we are raping the seas to please our stomachs without giving thought to conservation or the future of sea life. We are all to blame. We buy what the fishmonger sells and tend to end up cooking the most common species that we have been used to eating all our lives.

> We need to diversify and experiment with our taste-buds, and it's up to us restaurateurs to convince the general public that other species of fish are just as tasty and versatile.

There are other fish in the sea, though, that taste like good old cod and those other species that are being exhausted. We need to diversify and experiment with our taste-buds, and it's up to us restaurateurs and wholesalers to turn other species, such as pollack, huss, and mackerel, into trendy pieces of fish, and to convince the general public that they are just as tasty and versatile.

Take monkfish, for example. Who would even dare to eat a fish with those looks? But we do, and we've made it a prime fish to cook with, which has given the fishermen other opportunities to make a living. Anyway, that's food for thought, but there is a chance to change if only you change the way you eat, because, unlike that of sheep and cows, fish reproduction cannot be controlled.

Fish is actually pretty simple to cook – in fact, the less we do to it in preparation the better. For me, grilling, pan-frying, or baking with some simple herbs, salt, and pepper is all that good-quality fish really needs. We do tend to overcook fish as well, which is perhaps where we are going wrong. Some fish, like salmon and sea trout, can be treated like meat and cooked pink, whereas most other fish will need cooking through, but only just. Unless you are preparing sashimi, that is! On that subject, sashimi that is, you would be amazed, if you don't already know, how the flavour changes between a piece of dead fresh raw fish and when it's cooked. When I go fishing I always take wasabi and soy sauce just in case I catch anything, because it's just something not to be missed, especially with, say, mackerel – a humble fish to most but a special one to those in the know. Scallops are another example of a delicious raw delicacy. We eat oysters raw, so why not other seafood like mussels and clams? It's all a matter of making that leap.

"Red wine with fish? Not in this house, squire.

To red wine with fish no gentleman can aspire.

Give me a crusty Chablis. A mouldy Muscadet.

'Pon my sole, sir, I'll have it no other way.

Red wine and fish ain't right. It gets my goat.

Next thing you'll offer is women the vote."

The Old Fart's Refrain

IT IS POSSIBLE TO DRINK ONLY WATER WITH MANY FOODS (if you are, say, unwell or recovering from a bout of over-indulgence), but fish and shellfish cry out, weep copious tears, for wine. Yet, though wine and the fruits of the sea cohere so well, they are jointly undermined by a gross slander – fish requires white wine, never red – and marred by a huge over-simplification – only crisp, fresh, young white wines work. But who could contemplate a dish of grilled prawns without a manzanilla sherry to hand; a green Thai fish curry without Alsatian Tokay Pinot Gris; a pan-fried hake steak with sherry sauce without seven-year-old Aussie Semillon? And these are just a few of the white wine/fish dish marriages

to unnerve the old farts. Yes, Chablis and Muscadet can handle grilled sole and raw oysters, but the world has so many other dazzling fish and shellfish dishes to offer.

And what of red wine with fish? One-word answer: heavenly. Let me give you some examples of bliss-filled relationships: sea bass with Barolo or Barbaresco; salmon steak with Cabernet Sauvignon; lightly chilled Ribera del Duero from Spain with grilled or fried hake; New Zealand Pinot Noir with mussels; and Cabernet Franc with prawns — not chillied or gingery, but a little spring onion is permissible. With many of the fish and vegetable stews I cook at home, I routinely serve a chilled red wine – sometimes it's a Romanian Pinot Noir, other times a Sicilian Merlot. Once, I braved a bottle of Madiran (a wonderfully earthy, tannicly ferocious, Pyrénéan red wine) with a saddle of monkfish with garlic and Italian bacon. It was accompanied by an olive and tomato sauce. The wine almost smiled at me from its glass, it was so happy.

But these are exceptions, I grant you. There are no hard and fast rules when it comes to matching wine and food , though most of the time it is true that white wines do suit shellfish and oily fish. Spicy ingredients and especially sauces do affect the wine. It is also true that the wines of Alsace – Gewurztraminer, Tokay Pinot Gris, Riesling, and Pinot Blanc – are not generally thought of as going with oriental fish dishes, but they do. Thai, Chinese, Indian, Indonesian, and Japanese dishes, especially those with complex saucing, are superb with such wines. I have remarked on this elsewhere in the book, but I cannot emphasize enough how finely suited to exotic fish dishes are the wines of Alsace and Germany.

Even an English white wine can be enhanced by an encounter with a dish of whelks and winkles when without them it would appear somewhat feeble, clichéd, and feckless. A fish cake, so innocent-sounding a confection, can, if it be like Mark's Le Caprice salmon with sorrel and anchovy essence, transform an otherwise sedate, inexpensive Chablis into a firecracker...

"So you like my fish cakes, then? I haven't included the recipe in this book, though, Malc."

"I know. I mention them because I think they serve as a warning that fish dishes are not so easy to match with wine as many people think. You chefs love sticking little time bombs in dishes like that."

Fillet of Sea Trout with Samphire and Cockles

SERVES 4

SEA TROUT, COCKLES, AND SAMPHIRE ARE ALL AVAILABLE THROUGHOUT THE SUMMER MONTHS, so why not cook them together? Fresh cockles can be as delicious as the best palourde clams, but you might be put off by the gritty things in polystyrene cups that are sold at the seaside. You could use clams instead, but do try them and ask your fishmonger to order them in advance. To avoid the cockles being sandy, soak them in a bowl of cold water for about an hour and give them a vigorous stir every so often, then rinse them again in clean water.

4 X 200g (7oz) FILLETS OF SEA TROUT, SKIN ON AND ANY SMALL BONES REMOVED | SALT AND FRESHLY GROUND WHITE PEPPER | SPLASH OF OLIVE OIL | 200g (7oz) COCKLES, WELL RINSED | 100ml (3½fl oz) WHITE WINE | 100ml (3½fl oz) FISH STOCK (SEE BELOW), OR A CORNER OF A FISH STOCK CUBE DISSOLVED IN THAT AMOUNT OF HOT WATER) | 200g (7oz) SAMPHIRE, TRIMMED OF WOODY STALKS | 50g (1¾oz) UNSALTED BUTTER

1. Lightly season the sea trout with salt and pepper. Heat a little oil in a large nonstick pan and fry the pieces, skin-side down first, for about 3 minutes on each side, until they are nicely coloured. If the fillets are very thick, you will need to finish them in a hot oven for another 5–6 minutes.

2. Meanwhile, give the cockles a final rinse and put them into a large pan with the white wine and fish stock. Cover with a tight-fitting lid and cook over a high heat until they begin to open, shaking the pan and giving them an occasional stir. Drain the cockles in a colander, reserving the liquid and pouring it back into the pan.

3. Boil to reduce the liquid by half, then add the samphire and butter. Return the cockles to the pan (they will not need seasoning as the samphire will do that) and stir well.

4. To serve, carefully remove the sea trout from the pan with a fish slice, and spoon the cockles, samphire, and liquid over the top.

FISH STOCK

Fish stock, depending on what you are using it for, should be made with good-quality white-fish bones, such as sole, turbot, and halibut. Fishmongers should normally have these knocking around. To obtain a nice clear stock, you can blanch the bones first by bringing them to the boil from cold water, and then refreshing them in cold water.

Long cooking won't necessarily improve the flavour; 20 minutes is long enough, otherwise the stock may become bitter and lose that freshness. I always like to save fish bones in the freezer, then you can make fish stock when you have enough, and freeze it in small usable quantities.

To make 1–1½ litres (1¾–2¾ pints) Put the following ingredients in a saucepan, cover with cold water, and bring to the boil: 2kg (4lb 8oz) white-fish bones, chopped; 2 leeks, cleaned and roughly chopped; 2 onions, peeled and roughly chopped, 2 sticks of celery, roughly chopped; half a lemon; 1tsp fennel seeds; 20 black peppercorns; a few sprigs of thyme; 1 bay leaf; and a handful of parsley or parsley stalks. Skim and simmer gently for 20 minutes, skimming occasionally. Strain through a fine-meshed sieve. Check the strength of flavour of the stock, and boil it to reduce it if it isn't strong enough. It's now ready use.

FILLET OF SEA TROUT WITH SAMPHIRE AND COCKLES

THERE IS A SURPRISING DELICACY ABOUT THIS DISH. By itself each ingredient is an understatement, elegant yet flavoursome, but in concert the overall effect is highly civilized, almost prim in its mannered demureness. A strong white wine – a Chardonnay too long in the wood, a late-picked Viognier with a strong character of windfall apricot about it – and the dish is overwhelmed. However, France offers white Graves and Hermitage Blanc (Gerard and Jean-Louis Chave); New Zealand parades Pinot Gris (Matua Valley); Australia flaunts its Semillon; and Spain, or more properly Catalonia, has Torres Viña Sol in the screwcapped bottle.

You may ask what advantage a screwcapped wine offers in these circumstances. Well, you must agree that any wine stoppered with a cork has a flavour agent sealing it which, for good or ill, contributes something to the liquid when poured. A cork is a piece of treated wood bark and each cork is an individual constituent of each wine, and so one bottle of wine will differ from another bottle of exactly the same wine if the wine is kept for any length of time. A screwcap confers a freshness which keeps its integrity longer. This is a most useful characteristic when pairing a wine with this dish as samphire needs freshness along with the cockles (yet too raw a freshness and the trout is disturbed). A cork can never be a neutral seal. It affects the wine whatever the good intentions of its producer. Screwcaps, if perfect, guarantee that the bottle a wine critic writes about and rates highly is the same as the one his or her readers buy. No cork can perform likewise, which is why, as a wine critic, I believe screwcaps have a lot going for them.

If all the wines recommended to go with this dish were so sealed, I would be a much happier bunny. At which point, you may ask something: how will the wines recommended here work if one's trout has no cockles or samphire? The answer is splendidly. Unless, of course, you were, insanely, to add a curry sauce. But, who in his or her right mind would do that?

WINE CHECKLIST

WHITE GRAVES (BORDEAUX – FRANCE)

HERMITAGE BLANC (RHONE – FRANCE)

PINOT GRIS (NEW ZEALAND)

SEMILLON (AUSTRALIA)

CATALONIA WHITE (SPAIN)

Bouillabaisse

SERVES 4-6

IN THE SOUTH OF FRANCE, THERE ARE MANY HEATED DISCUSSIONS ABOUT WHAT SHOULD GO INTO A BOUILLABAISSE. In Marseilles, the home of the dish, there is bitter rivalry between chefs over who makes the best and most authentic. Traditionally, it is made with rascasse and weever – ugly-looking rockfish – conger eel, gurnard, and other fish such as John Dory. Some of these classic bouillabaisse fish are caught here in England, and if you ask the local fishermen they might well be glad to get rid of them. You can also use huss, or dogfish as the fishermen call it, and bulk it up with mussels and chunks of lobster if you are feeling indulgent.

I love the idea of cooking what's available from a good fishmonger – just grabbing a selection of fish and making a fish stew in a bouillabaisse style. This way, you can use the head and bones to make a rich fish-soup base and use chunks of fillets or cuts through the bone in the stew. Ideally, you want to cut everything, including any shellfish you are using, into pieces that will take the same time to cook as each other. The most important thing, though, is to have a good base, but if you are short of time there are some good fish soups on the market.

2 TBSP **OLIVE OIL** | 1 KG (2 LB 4 OZ) **FISH, GUTTED AND CHOPPED INTO SMALL CHUNKS – HEAD, TAILS, SCALES, AND ALL BONY BITS INCLUDED** | 1 MEDIUM ONION, ROUGHLY CHOPPED | 1 LEEK, ROUGHLY CHOPPED | 1 SMALL FENNEL BULB, TRIMMED AND ROUGHLY CHOPPED | 1 RED PEPPER, DESEEDED AND ROUGHLY CHOPPED | 6 CLOVES GARLIC, CHOPPED | 1 MEDIUM POTATO, PEELED AND ROUGHLY CHOPPED | 1 BAY LEAF | A FEW SPRIGS OF THYME | GOOD PINCH OF SAFFRON | 1 TSP BLACK PEPPERCORNS | 3 JUNIPER BERRIES | 1 TBSP **TOMATO PUREE** | 1 X 400 G TIN CHOPPED TOMATOES | 100 ML (3½ FL OZ) RED WINE | 4 LITRES (7 PINTS) FISH STOCK (SEE PAGE 57) | SALT AND FRESHLY GROUND BLACK PEPPER
TO SERVE
1½ KG (3 LB 5 OZ) SELECTION OF FISH SUCH AS HUSS, RED MULLET, AND GURNARD, CUT THROUGH THE BONE OR FILLETS (ALLOW ABOUT 400 G/14 OZ FISH ON THE BONE PER PERSON) | 8 SLICES FRENCH BREAD, TOASTED | 80 G (2¾ OZ) GRUYERE CHEESE, GRATED

1. Heat the olive oil in a large heavy-based pan and gently fry the fish, vegetables, herbs, saffron, peppercorns, and berries for about 10 minutes. Add the tomato purée, chopped tomatoes, wine, and fish stock. Bring to the boil, season with salt and pepper, and simmer for 50 minutes.

2. Blend about one third of the soup in a liquidizer (bones and all) and return to the pan. Simmer gently for another 20 minutes. Strain the soup through a sieve and check again for seasoning.

3. Return the soup to the pan and simmer once again. Add the pieces of fish. Robust fish such as huss will stand a little overcooking and can be simmered for 10 minutes; flaky fish needs only 5–6 minutes.

Serve with toasted French bread and grated Gruyère.

BOUILLABAISSE

ONE OF THE FIERCEST BOUILLABAISSES I WAS EVER OFFERED WAS IN A VILLAGE BY A LAKE OUTSIDE MARSEILLES, and the wine was a Bouches du Rhône Blanc of sufficient acidic *oomph* to clean rusty armour. By twisting my host's arm I was granted leave to acquire a local rosé, but this was too weedy to cope. What I craved, and recommend as one approach with Mark's style of bouillabaisse, is indeed a rosé and, though there are many candidates, I am taken most with Cabernet Sauvignon Rosé from Chile and Hungary. However, there are two Aussie whites which also go well, both from the same producer, and each bears a proud screwcap to retain all the wine's freshness, texture, and bite. They are D'Arenberg Hermit Crab Marsanne/Viognier and D'Arenberg Olive Grove Chardonnay.

Aussie Chardonnays, in days past, exhibited a buttery boisterousness which is out of place with this dish. This flavour was not so much a function of any wood ageing as the strong character given by the manipulation in the winery of the secondary, malolactic fermentation. Malolactic fermentation is what happens when the wine's natural acids are allowed to change from malic, which is sharp and appley, to lactic, which is milky and soft. For years, Australian Chardonnays were characterized by an enthusiasm for a high percentage of malolactic fermentation. Modern examples are crisper and suit subtler dishes as a result.

My other choice of wine for this dish is Chilean Chardonnay from Casablanca. Ignacio Recabarren's Casablanca Chardonnay Santa Isabel Estate was an instant hit with me when I tasted, in Chile, the first vintage back in the mid-1990s. This wine is a superb fish partner – and it is interesting that its maker, his searching amber eyes alive with interest, was as keen to discuss such an aspect of it as he was to reveal the finer points of its crafting. He is now winemaker at Concha y Toro as well as running his own winery.

"I have lived in this area for ten years," he told me. "I taste the grapes all the time. The same sort of flaws you get in the mouth when you taste the grape you get in the finished wines. So I grow perfect grapes and let these grapes call the shots. The idea behind all my Casablanca wines are to express fruit – no malolactic fermentation, little wood."

And that's what we want in a wine to go with this dish: pure fruit with integrity. This is a feature of my last, and perhaps most luxurious, choice of wine for this dish: Châteauneuf-du-Pape Blanc. This product of Grenache Blanc, Clairette, Bourboulenc, and possibly Roussanne can be magnificent with just a couple of years of bottle-age (in spite of those corks). Rayas, Vieux Télégraphe, Beaucastel, Nalys, Clos des Papes, Gardine, and Mont Redon are names to look for.

WINE CHECKLIST

CABERNET SAUVIGNON ROSE (CHILE AND HUNGARY)

MARSANNE/VIOGNIER BLEND (SOUTH AUSTRALIA)

CHARDONNAY (SOUTH AUSTRALIA AND CASABLANCA VALLEY – CHILE)

CHATEAUNEUF-DU-PAPE BLANC (RHONE – FRANCE)

Grilled Sardines on Toast

SERVES 4 AS A STARTER

BRING BACK PILCHARDS, I SAY. In fact, they are back. It's just that no one wants to buy them, but they will buy sardines. Well, I've got news for you: the pilchard is a grown-up sardine whether you like it or not.

2 SHALLOTS, FINELY CHOPPED | 6TBSP EXTRA-VIRGIN OLIVE OIL, PLUS EXTRA FOR BRUSHING | 3 RIPE TOMATOES, SKINNED, DESEEDED, AND CUT INTO ROUGH 1CM (½ INCH) DICE | 1TBSP CHOPPED PARSLEY | SALT AND FRESHLY GROUND BLACK PEPPER | 2TSP WHITE WINE VINEGAR | 6 SARDINES, FILLETED AND BONES REMOVED | 4 THICK SLICES OF BREAD

1. Gently cook the shallots in the olive oil for 2–3 minutes without colouring. Add the tomatoes and parsley, season well, and cook for another couple of minutes. Remove from the heat, stir in the vinegar, and put to one side.

2. Meanwhile, heat the grill to its highest setting. Make a couple of diagonal slashes across each fillet, then brush with olive oil, and season. Grill the fish for about 3–4 minutes skin-side up.

3. Toast the bread on both sides. To serve, arrange the sardines on the bread and spoon the warm tomato mixture over the top.

OILY FISH

Great British oily fish such as mackerel, herring, and sprats have now been forgotten. These types of fish were once our staple and were cured by smoking, salting, and pickling to preserve for trading and eating out of season. It's a shame the cheaper fish are slightly frowned upon, but aren't kippers, soused mackerel, and maybe those tinned pilchards just great eats?

Believe it or not, over a century or so ago, there was serious tuna fishing going on off the UK's east coast and that was purely because they would feed off oily fish such as the herring, which have now almost disappeared from our coastlines.

You hear stories now, though, of big-eye tuna being caught off the south coast, which sounds like a freak occurrence, but might be the result of global warming and species migrating into warmer waters. We might even hear more of these stories.

Anyway, we need to incorporate more oily fish into our diet, because – apart from all the health reasons – it's delicious. You would probably think nothing of ordering sardines when you were on the coast in the Mediterranean, though you would run your eyes straight past the offer of pilchards or sprats over here, but they are actually the same species and equally good.

GRILLED SARDINES ON TOAST

THIS CUNNINGLY CONTRIVED DISH, WHERE OILINESS COMPETES WITH ACIDITY, fruitiness with vegetal herbiness, is a nightmare for any wine that is not as keen as a sushi chef's knife. Sharpness, though, is not tartness. It is a freshness, often tinged with minerality; it is an immediacy of citrusiness; it is a pleasing grapiness, as if the wine truly does exude the air of having been squeezed from fresh fruit.

The ingredients delight in New Zealand Sauvignon Blancs and Rieslings. Individually, each ingredient matches a separate wine. The shallots delight in Semillons from the Hunter Valley in Australia. The tomatoes adore one of those Rhône whites composed of Bourboulenc, Colombard, a touch of Viognier, perhaps. The sardines, unadorned, enjoy the genteel *pétillance* of Portuguese Vinho Verde – a wine so fresh and gurgly it is not so much uncorked as unnapped – but also take to Chablis, Muscadet, Savennières, the really dry Cape Chenin Blancs, and unoaked Chardonnays from Western and South Australia.

But put all that together and what do we have? A blend that is impossible to contemplate, let alone find. We must, therefore, settle on one, two or perhaps three, of these. These would be Shingle Peak Riesling or Wither Hills Sauvignon Blanc from New Zealand or a Sauvignon Blanc from Chile. We got there in the end. But there is also a strong Aussie candidate: Knappstein Hand Picked Riesling from the Clare Valley. So any of our candidate wines go well with that humble piece of toast with its princely sardines aboard.

WINE CHECKLIST

SAUVIGNON BLANC (MARLBOROUGH – NEW ZEALAND AND CHILE)

RIESLING (NEW ZEALAND AND CLARE VALLEY – SOUTH AUSTRALIA)

VINHO VERDE (NORTH PORTUGAL)

CHABLIS (BURGUNDY – FRANCE)

MUSCADET (LOIRE – FRANCE)

SAVENNIERES (LOIRE – FRANCE)

CHENIN BLANC (SOUTH AFRICA)

UNOAKED CHARDONNAY (WESTERN AND SOUTH AUSTRALIA)

WINE AND OILY FISH
The key to getting a wine to work with oily fish is to always remember that the oiliness can boost certain wines' freshness and acidic bite. This is where the wines chosen have an edge: they have bite.

Sole Véronique

SERVES 4

CLASSIC DISHES ARE MAKING A COMEBACK, and I remember this one from a live cookery competition I entered when I first arrived in London as a commis chef. Just to make it really difficult, the rule was that it had to be the ultimate classic recipe according to Escoffier: no cream in the recipe, just butter; and the dish had to be glazed under a hot grill with no egg yolk or anything. I just about got away with it, but most ended up with a plate of oily fish and grapes. One of our regulars, Nancy McLarty, who unfortunately died a few years back, would occasionally request Sole Véronique. We adapted the recipe for her as she had a bit of a tricky diet, to say the least. Dover sole is a classic in this recipe, but it will work equally well with any firm-fleshed white fish.

600–650G (1LB 5OZ–1LB 7OZ) DOVER SOLE FILLETS, SKINNED AND TRIMMED | SALT AND FRESHLY GROUND WHITE PEPPER | 50ML (2FL OZ) WHITE WINE | 1TBSP CURACAO | 500ML (18FL OZ) FISH STOCK | 400ML (14FL OZ) DOUBLE CREAM | 1 EGG YOLK | 40 SEEDLESS WHITE GRAPES, PEELED

1. Score each of the sole fillets 4 or 5 times with a sharp knife on the side that was attached to the bone. Fold them in half and score them on the fold to avoid curling up when cooked. You can, if you fancy a different presentation, tie each fillet into a knot.

Season the fillets and put them into a pan with the wine, curaçao, and fish stock. Cover with greaseproof paper, pushing it onto the fillets and tight to the edges of the pan. Bring to a slow boil, simmer for 2 minutes, then remove from the heat.

2. Remove the fillets with a slotted spoon and keep them warm, covered with the greaseproof paper, in a very low oven. Boil the liquid to reduce down to about 4–5 tablespoons. Add the cream, bring back to the boil, and simmer until it has reduced by about two thirds and thickened enough to coat the back of a spoon.

Meanwhile, put the egg yolk in a small bowl with about a tablespoon of the sauce. Whisk it over a pan of simmering water until it becomes light and frothy – it will only take a minute.

3. Heat a grill to its highest setting. Taste the sauce and season if necessary. Add the grapes to the sauce and stir in the egg until well combined. Drain any liquid from the sole fillets, and put them into a heatproof serving dish or on individual heat resistant plates. Spoon the sauce and grapes over the fish and glaze under the grill until golden.

Serve with buttered spinach, spring vegetables, and new potatoes.

WHITE FISH

Depending on the freshness, most white fish can be adapted to suit recipes, except perhaps those involving char-grilling. Fish such as plaice will stand up to heavy-duty cooking the bigger they get, but the smaller one-portion fish tend to flake when grilled. We buy large, diver-caught plaice in the restaurants, and they come in the size of a good turbot or brill at times. They are great fish, and their flesh has a completely different texture and flavour from that of their siblings. Fish like pollack are much the same; a large pollack of say 4–5kg will taste as good as a cod – and, of course, there's less on your conscience that way.

SOLE VERONIQUE

NEVER DID SO INNOCENT-SOUNDING A DISH ILLUSTRATE SO VIVIDLY THE PROBLEMS OF WORKING WITH CHEFS WITH BRILLIANT IDEAS. Curaçao? A wicked intervention if ever there was one, for curaçao refers to an orange liqueur named after an island off the Venezuelan coast, and it has been around for some centuries. Its presence adds a dimension we must consider if we are to find the right wine.

Véronique is a bit of a bitch. The sauce is middling-rich, counterpointed by the acids of the grapes and the curaçao. This suggests we need a white wine with sufficient weight to handle the bustle of that sauce, but not too robust (as a Californian Chardonnay might be, and certainly a Barossa Chardonnay by itself) for the delicacy of the fish. A Savennières from the Loire – a dry Chenin Blanc – is one interesting answer.

Another, and this is my premier candidate, is Aussie Semillon – if you can find one with one or two years, preferably four or five, of bottle-age, we are looking at a to-die-for union of food and wine. A McLaren Vale Semillon from an estate such as Coriole would be magnificent, but more choice is offered if we visit the Lower Hunter Valley and look for specific names: Scarborough, Tamburlaine, and Tyrrell's. But there are many others, and I do believe this is this region's great white wine style. With maturity, five or six years maybe, or eight in some instances, the wine is at its peak and utterly superb, providing oily richness with swirling citrusy minerals. Another interesting option for this dish would be a Californian Pinot Noir from the Marimar Torres estate.

WINE CHECKLIST

SAVENNIERES (LOIRE – FRANCE)

SEMILLON (LOWER HUNTER VALLEY, BAROSSA VALLEY, AND MCLAREN VALE – AUSTRALIA)

PINOT NOIR (CALIFORNIA – THE USA)

WINE AND WHITE FISH

Plain cooked fish is wonderful because it is expressive of nothing but itself – a sea freshness where there is a subtle aroma and none of the salinity or brininess that comes from fish that has been disguised (or enhanced) with a sauce.

A strong wine will overwhelm it. With grilled fish, an unwooded Aussie Chardonnay is superb, as is Riesling from the Clare Valley. Chablis has always been thought of as classic partner, but a fine, whistle-clean one is required. English wine can cope as well, too. However, in many ways it is the more obscure white wines of Europe that clamour for partnership with this kind of fish: Alvarinho from Spain, Gavi from northern Italy, Pinot Blanc from Alsace, Savignin from the Jura, Hungarian Sauvignon Blanc, Côtes du Rhône (made from the Marsanne, Roussanne, and Bourboulenc grapes) and – the *crème de la crème* in this context – Picpoul de Pinet from the Languedoc in France. A fish cooked with or without herb butter and/or lemon will happily settle down with Sauvignon Blanc, citrusy Chardonnay or Viognier.

Smoked Mackerel Salad with Poached Egg

SERVES 4

THERE ARE VARIOUS QUALITIES OF SMOKED MACKEREL ON THE MARKET, and most of the ones I've tried seem to be of a fairly good quality, as mackerel itself is quite an oily fish and withstands even the severest of smokings.

1TBSP **VEGETABLE OIL** | 2TBSP **OLIVE OIL** | 2 SLICES OF BREAD, CUT INTO ROUGH 1CM (½ INCH) CUBES | 1 SMALL HEAD OF FRISÉE LETTUCE (ABOUT 150G/5½OZ), TRIMMED, WASHED, AND TORN | SALT AND FRESHLY GROUND BLACK PEPPER | 2 SMOKED MACKEREL FILLETS, SKINNED, BONES REMOVED, AND FLAKED INTO CHUNKS | 4 MEDIUM EGGS
FOR THE DRESSING
1TSP **FRESHLY GRATED HORSERADISH OR HORSERADISH SAUCE** | 1TBSP **GOOD-QUALITY TARRAGON VINEGAR** | 2TSP **DIJON MUSTARD** | 1 CLOVE GARLIC, CRUSHED | 2TBSP **OLIVE OIL** | 2TBSP **VEGETABLE OR CORN OIL**

1. First, make the dressing. Put all the ingredients into a clean bottle or jar. Give it a good shake and leave to infuse overnight at room temperature.

2. Heat the vegetable and olive oil in a frying pan and fry the bread cubes for 1–2 minutes, turning a few times until evenly coloured. Drain on kitchen paper. Dress the salad leaves with half the dressing and season.

3. Arrange the salad on four plates with the mackerel and croûtons. Poach the eggs until soft, then drain on kitchen paper and place in the centre of the salad. Spoon a little more dressing over and serve.

PICKLED AND PRESERVED FISH

Gravadlax, soused mackerel, pickled herring, and marinated anchovies are all good examples of old-fashioned ways of preserving fish, before we had the luxury of refrigeration. We have held onto these old techniques over the centuries and adapted them to modern eating styles. In some cases, we have kept them exactly as they would have been served – and why not? You can't beat a good brandade or pickled herring. The great thing about preserving is that it gives the fish a completely new flavour and texture, and for cooking it means new recipes and new creations.

I remember years ago stopping off in a restaurant in the country on the way to Barcelona. There was no menu, and one of the courses was, I thought, tripe with girolle mushrooms. It turned out to be trippa de bacalau, which is salted cod belly. It was delicious, but what it did was give a cut that would normally have been binned a new dimension.

SMOKED MACKEREL SALAD WITH POACHED EGG

THERE IS AN ABUNDANCE OF CANDIDATE WINES – a plethora, truth to tell – that clamour for consideration with this dish. I would certainly not protest if Mark's mackerel was being served up with any of the white wines recommended for any of the preceding fish dishes. However, we want perfection, do we not? We demand unerring, precise perfection.

We shall, then, take a trip to the Cape of Good Hope in South Africa. The first wine under consideration, getting us close to perfection, is the cheeky Rhône-style white called Goats do Roam, made by Charles Back at the Fairview Estate. Splendid yes, but not as biting, incisive, or concentrated as the one wine (or rather two) I wish to see, above all, beside this dish: Springfield Estate Life from Stone Sauvignon Blanc, and Springfield Estate Special Cuvée Sauvignon Blanc, both of which are made by Abrie Bruwer in Robertson. The first of these exhibits such an extruded citrusy tanginess that it is sublime with the mackerel. The second Springfield wine has more mineral bounce (that some might argue the dressing in the dish will flatten). Nonetheless, I press the claims of the Sauvignons from this estate for prime consideration with this mackerel. Springfield is one of the most serious, yet happiest, wine estates I have ever come across.

It is possible to be committed yet not fanatical, detached yet not insular, wild without being wacky, and humane without being sentimental – the remarkable Springfield estate echoes all of these things, and it is a delight to taste its liquids and tour the vines. Best of all, though, is to have its Sauvignons alongside this mackerel dish. For however attractive a vineyard, however seductive its proprietors, if its wines don't work with the dish in front of you, something is wrong. It is, I suppose, something this book has been designed to put right.

WINE CHECKLIST

SAUVIGNON BLANC (ROBERTSON – SOUTH AFRICA)

RHONE-STYLE BLEND (PAARL – SOUTH AFRICA)

WINE AND PICKLED AND PRESERVED FISH

Let me first get out of the way the definition of pickled (wine writers know all about the condition). Fish which are cured, such as smoked salmon, or eel, are not "pickled", and are out of my remit in this section except for me to remark, in passing, that such dishes are superb with Californian Chardonnays.

Pickling is usually death to any wine as the very name of the preserving agent, vinegar, comes from *vin aigre* – sour wine. Pickled herrings, rollmops, winkles, and whelks go only, if at all, with Retsina from Greece. They also, in a rare admission for me, go with wheat beers and certain lagers (Czech ones especially). Escabeche, the great Spanish fish dish, where the fish is fried before being laid in a marinade of vinegar with spices, can work with wine. White Riojas from Spain, not too old, not too oaky, are perfect.

Steamed Scallops and Tiger Prawns with Ginger and Spring Onions

SERVES 4 AS A STARTER

AS A KID IN WEST BAY IN DORSET I WORKED IN A PUB ON THE QUAYSIDE AND OFTEN GOT BOXES FULL OF SCALLOPS IN THE SHELL. Unfortunately, I was a bit green around the ears and didn't really have a mentor to look up to; I used to completely massacre them and cook them for four times as long as I should have. Oh well, we live and learn, but I do like the way the Chinese prepare scallops – just simple, with no fuss and brief cooking.

4 LARGE OR 8 SMALL, HEADLESS TIGER PRAWNS, DEVEINED AND SHELLED, TAILS INTACT | 4 LARGE SCALLOPS OR 8 MEDIUM ONES, CLEANED, IN THE CUPPED HALF SHELLS | SALT AND FRESHLY GROUND WHITE PEPPER | 40G (1½OZ) ROOT GINGER, PEELED AND FINELY SHREDDED | 6 SPRING ONIONS, SHREDDED ON THE ANGLE | 2 CLOVES GARLIC, FINELY CHOPPED | 1TBSP LIGHT SOY SAUCE | GOOD HANDFUL OF SEAWEED (OPTIONAL) | A FEW SPRIGS OF CORIANDER

1. Put a tiger prawn (or two) into each shell with the scallops, season with a little salt and pepper, and scatter the ginger, spring onion, and garlic over them. Spoon a little soy into each shell, and cover each one with foil.

2. Steam for 4–5 minutes in a steamer, or you can use a roasting tray, with a couple of centimetres of boiling water covered with a lid or foil, set on the hob.

3. Arrange the shells on a little seaweed, if you can get it, to stop them wobbling around, then add a sprig or so of coriander to each.

ASIAN-INFLUENCED DISHES

Isn't it great the way food trends are forever changing? Suddenly we are all experts on Asian food and know the restaurant lingo. I suppose holidays to Asian countries are on the up, and can be a great help when trying to decipher a menu back home. These days we can pick up Asian herbs and spices quite easily in greengrocers and supermarkets, which makes the ever-popular Asian cuisine easier to recreate at home.

Years ago, we struggled unless we had an Asian supermarket nearby, but now we can knock up a Thai curry, for example, with complete authenticity. Even the tiny pea aubergines seem as widely available as galangal and lemon grass. To make it all the more authentic, you can top up your crockery set with traditional bowls, plates, and platters.

Asian-influenced food is creeping onto restaurant menus, and often will quite comfortably sit next to something completely classic like, say, a braised beef dish in Guinness.

STEAMED SCALLOPS AND TIGER PRAWNS WITH GINGER AND SPRING ONIONS

THE ENTRY IN MY OLD NOTEBOOK IS RATHER VAGUE: D93 BETWEEN PRIVAS AND CREST where the river Drome meets the river Rhône, at a place called Livron. This is where I was directed to find the small appellation whence comes the unusual white wine in the photograph: Brézème. At the time, I was en route to Provence to a wedding, and distractions attendant upon this union meant I did never get to Livron and taste Brézème Blanc on its home turf (as few people, including locals, ever do).

Brézème is one of the smallest and least known appellations in France, and I discovered it some years back when a single, brave, British wine merchant, Robin Yapp of Yapp Bros (now succeeded by his son Jason), stocked the rarity. And though it was the red I first tried, described by its doughty importer as "a hairy beast, reekingly animal, pungently tannic", the white, usually a Marsanne/Viognier blend, always struck me as having, more than the other white Rhône wines touched on in this book, a peculiarly civilized rustic demeanour and unabashed *élan*.

It's a wonderfully confident wine with a dish like this, which has traps for the unwary wine waiter with that ginger and spring onion. Yet scallops, being delicate, can be overwhelmed by a strong white, and though Brézème is characterful it seems to extend a light touch as it caresses the palate, and the dish impacts the taste-buds, and the liquid enhances the food and vice versa. If, however, you overdo the ginger in this dish then the wine's satin texture will be ruffled, and in these circumstances I must recommend a wine from the same stable as the wine I so enthusiastically recommended with the smoked mackerel salad.

This is Springfield Estate Méthode Ancienne Unfiltered Chardonnay, made by Abrie Bruwer in the Cape, using wild yeast native to the winery (unlike wines which have been inoculated with a commercial yeast to initiate the ferment from grape fluid into alcohol). "Ach, the longevity of wild yeast wines!" exclaimed Abrie, as he once explained to me his affection for this wine. I am only slightly embarrassed to report that my tasting notes for this wine, made some time after having consumed the best part of a bottle read: "It is gorgeous, wild, lengthy, and sensual – something like a poem by Baudelaire, a bit like a Mozart Piano Sonata." Such a wine is not going to be fazed by ginger or spring onion, and yet it will handle those fragile scallops.

WINE CHECKLIST

BREZEME COTES DU RHONE WHITE (RHONE – FRANCE)

CHARDONNAY (ROBERTSON – SOUTH AFRICA)

Moules Marinières

SERVES 4

YOU CAN GET MUSSELS ALL YEAR ROUND, although, like oysters, when the water is warm they get broody and will not be at their best for eating, and you may be disappointed. Autumn and throughout the winter is the time to buy them, and usually these days they will be ready cleaned of barnacles. A little cream can be added to a classic moules marinières, but the choice is yours.

1 MEDIUM ONION, FINELY CHOPPED | 6 MEDIUM CLOVES GARLIC, CRUSHED | GLASS OF MEDIUM WHITE WINE | 150ML (5FL OZ) FISH STOCK | SALT AND FRESHLY GROUND BLACK PEPPER | 2KG (4LB 8OZ) LIVE MUSSELS, SCRUBBED AND BEARDS REMOVED | 2TBSP CHOPPED PARSLEY

1. Put the onion, garlic, wine, and fish stock into a large saucepan and bring to the boil. Meanwhile, discard any mussels that stay open when tapped.

2. Season the liquid and add the mussels and parsley. Cover with a lid and cook on a high heat, stirring occasionally, until all the mussels have opened (one or two may not, but don't keep cooking, just discard the closed ones). Serve immediately.

PARSLEY

The humble parsley, probably the most common of herbs, often gets abused and just scattered over food to give it some colour. Well, I'm afraid it just doesn't do it any justice when it's there to garnish and not to complement the dish in any way. Both flat and curly parsley have excellent uses in the kitchen for their flavour and aroma. For me, a good old parsley sauce, whether it be for a boiled leg of mutton or a piece of steamed fish, is a fine thing. Again, its purpose is not to be thrown into the sauce at the last minute, but to be simmered for a few minutes to give the sauce that fragrant garden flavour.

In salads, it also has its uses. I like to use young leaves of flat parsley, just picked, washed, and tossed in a green salad. One of the salads that people just can't get their heads around is tabbouleh – even my chefs sometimes struggle because they haven't experienced the real thing. A visit to a Lebanese restaurant will reveal that the salad needs ninety-five per cent roughly chopped flat parsley and mint, to five per cent cracked wheat. Yes, that's a hell of a lot of parsley and mint, and it's not one of those salads where you can get lazy and throw in extra cracked wheat.

MOULES MARINIERES

A ONE-LINE ANSWER SUFFICES: DRINK WITH THE DISH THE WHITE WINE YOU USE AS ONE OF ITS INGREDIENTS. This is not because of some holy or holistic attitude on my part. It is not because it is the easy answer. It is because thinking of the wine in that way concentrates the mind on the fact that the wine in the dish must be good enough to drink and is not an any-old-bottle which can be dismissed as a mere ingredient. Why should you cook using mediocre components? You wouldn't use mouldy carrots or stale garlic, would you? Indeed, one habit I have long had is to sip the wine I am using in the cooking whilst I am doing the cooking. In the instance of this dish, the list of candidate bottles is long. Too dry and the richness of those bivalve molluscs will overpower it; too fruity and there is a jarring of elements. Not that a degree of fruitiness in the wine isn't necessary, but it must be in keeping – not too woody, not over-spicy.

I would say that, more than with most dishes, the wine accompanying moules marinières is so important an ingredient that it actually shapes the way the dish can perform on the palate. Therefore, if you want a luxurious yet characterful feel with the dish, choose an aged Aussie Semillon such as Scarborough or Tyrrell's. If you want a more rustic feel, go for a young Muscadet or a Picpoul de Pinet from the Languedoc. If you want aromatic precision, then it has to be a Sauvignon Blanc from Marlborough in New Zealand. Silky luxuriousness? Then choose an unoaked Chardonnay from Australia or a lightly oaked Californian Chardonnay such as Bonterra from the organic vineyards of Fetzer in Hopland. The list is literally endless and even encompasses wines from the UK – a choice largely restricted to the residents of that place, to which natives of more benign climates may respond "thank the Almighty". However, there are half a dozen drinkable English and Welsh wines, and English mussels can be superb. My first choice English wine is from Gloucestershire's Three Choirs Vineyard.

All of the wines in this list will also work well with mussels cooked in various other ways. However, if a subtle degree of spiciness is involved, then choose the keenest edged whites, Picpoul de Pinet and the New Zealand Sauvignon Blanc. If ginger is used, or lemon grass, then go for the fuller wines, the Semillons and Chardonnays.

WINE CHECKLIST

SEMILLON (NEW SOUTH WALES – AUSTRALIA)

MUSCADET (LOIRE – FRANCE)

PICPOUL DE PINET (LANGUEDOC – FRANCE)

SAUVIGNON BLANC (MARLBOROUGH – NEW ZEALAND)

UNOAKED CHARDONNAY (AUSTRALIA)

CHARDONNAY (MENDOCINO – CALIFORNIA)

ENGLISH WHITE (GLOUCESTERSHIRE – ENGLAND)

WINE AND PARSLEY
This herb is often used with the shellfish and has little effect on any wine, except an excess of it seems to favour fruity whites like Tokay Pinot Gris or Gewurztraminer or a full-on Aussie Chardonnay.

Sashimi

SERVES 1+

WE ARE COMING ROUND TO THE IDEA AT LAST OF EATING FISH IN ITS PUREIST FORM – RAW. Okay, it may take you some time to get your head round it, but once you've tried it, there's no looking back. Within hours of being caught is obviously the best way, and whenever I go fishing these days my tackle bag always contains soy, pickled ginger, and wasabi.

I was sailing in the Solent last year on my friend's yacht and couldn't resist casting a fly into shoals of mackerel whilst the sails were up. The other hardened sailers must have thought we were bonkers, but I bet they weren't eating sashimi an hour later!

Most fish and shellfish are suitable for eating raw as long as they are ultra fresh and you can trust your fishmonger's judgement. Certain flat fish such as flounder, plaice, and skate are not that suitable. Some are better for eating than others and it's very much down to personal preference. The thought of raw sea urchin to some people is repulsive and to others heavenly. I remember asking some divers in Ireland to grab us some sea urchins. "What for?" was the reply, but we did eventually persuade them.

Wasabi quality varies dramatically from cheap, tasteless, dull green stuff in tubes to the powdered variety. If you are lucky enough to find it, the fresh root is the best, which can be grated on little, hand-made, sharkskin graters.

ALLOW ABOUT 90G (3¼0Z) SKINNED FISH FILLET PER PERSON | WASABI | SOY SAUCE | GRATED DAIKON (WHITE RADISH) | PICKLED GINGER

1. Start by preparing the fish. Remove any bones and rinse away any blood. With a very sharp knife, cut the fish fillets across at an angle into 2.5cm (1 inch) slices, ¼–½cm thick.

2. Arrange the fish in a neat line on a (preferably Oriental-style) platter, and serve the accompaniments in little piles on the plate or in individual bowls.

JAPANESE-INFLUENCED DISHES

Until Nobu arrived in London, the habit of eating Japanese food in the UK was restricted to those in the know or maybe those with a tip-off about a little backstreet treasure that only the Japanese frequented. Today, a quick shopping trip can coincide with a brief taste of Japan by means of the ever-increasing Sushi-bar chains that pop up in department stores and high streets everywhere. You even see young kids munching away at raw fish as it rotates in front of them.

It's probably the one type of food that appeals to most, whether it's for a quick, light snack, an expensive blowout, or a healthy substitute for mainstream restaurants. You can see the appeal: it's a clean and healthy way to eat, it's got style, and it's got theatre and art in its preparation and presentation. You can even watch the skilfully trained sushi chefs at work, preparing your meal.

SASHIMI

AN AROMATIC, CRISP, DRY WHITE WINE WITH AN UNDERLYING SENSE OF PURPOSE AND PURITY; perhaps grapiness is one way to express it. That is one school of thought (the wine to work with the raw fish approach). Another is a white wine with a degree of oiliness to its texture. But then there is the third way; this takes note of the two most astringently delicious components in the dish – the wasabi and that pickled ginger.

The wine that works best is undoubtedly – and this may be a surprise – something late-picked. It could be a Tokay Pinot Gris from Alsace. It could be a Spätlese Riesling from the Rhine, Nahe, or Mosel. But it could also be a late-harvested Chenin Blanc from the Cape produced by Ken and Theresa Forrester of Scholtzenhof Farm just outside Stellenbosch. Most startling of the wines from here, and there is an impressive line of dry reds and whites, is the sweetest: a Noble Late Harvest Botrytised Chenin Blanc, the honeyed richness and elegant acidity of which will see the wine through the next thirty years. Sashimi goes wonderfully with sweet Chenin as long as it has a high level of acidity, which the Chenin Blanc grape produces naturally, for this is necessary to counteract not only the soy sauce and that green mustard but also, above all, the pickled ginger.

The great Chenin Blancs of the Loire, it follows logically, especially the Vouvrays, are superb with sashimi (and sushi), but not the *sec* or the *demi-sec* styles (otherwise brilliant tipples). This dish demands the sweeter Vouvrays, characterized as *moelleux* (and one name to pay particular attention to is Huët, the organic producer). *Moelleux* means soft and creamy, more or less, but with a wine it denotes a sweeter or half-sweet style. The late-picked whites of Alsace, and the Spätlese Rieslings of the Mosel, are also good choices with this dish. In Alsace, look for Zind-Humbrecht, Kuentz-Bas, Kientzler, Weinbach, Becker, and Humbrecht. In the Mosel, go for von Kesselstatt, von Schubert, Paulinshof, and Willi Haag.

WINE CHECKLIST

TOKAY PINOT GRIS (ALSACE – FRANCE)

RIESLING SPATLESE (RHINE, NAHE, MOSEL – GERMANY)

LATE-HARVEST CHENIN BLANC (STELLENBOSCH – SOUTH AFRICA)

VOUVRAY MOELLEUX (LOIRE – FRANCE)

VENDANGE TARDIVE (ALSACE – FRANCE)

3
Meat

WHATEVER MAKES THE HEADLINES, WE ARE CARNIVORES AT HEART. Well, except for a few vegetarians, pescatarians, and the ones who suddenly become vegetarians when the menu is plonked in front of them. There are also vegetarians who eat chicken, but I'm really not sure which category they fit into.

The more we know about food, the more we want to know the provenance of what we are buying. The word "organic" creeps into this way of buying quite often, but, although this tells us how the animals have been brought up, it's quite often not reflected in the taste and texture of the end product.

I'm all for organic eating, but if the quality is not up to it, then what's the point? If someone describes an Aberdeen Angus and Longhorn crossbreed that's lived its life grazing on grass and heather on the surrounding hills of Loch Fyne in Scotland as having flavour and texture that are second to none, then that's good enough for me. Likewise, if a Blackface lamb or mutton with a good pedigree and upbringing crosses my path, it needs not to be deemed organic for the sake of it. Its flavour is what it needs to

qualify for a place on the menu or in my fridge at home. Cooking methods and knowledge can also counteract all of the above. You can take home the best of the best in your shopping basket and cremate it completely, and lose everything you set out to achieve, except, perhaps, that peace of mind.

I've been to dinner parties where the host has gone out of his or her way to buy expensive produce, and not done it any justice whatsoever in the preparation and cooking. I've had to ask myself: "What's the point?"

The more we know about food, the more we want to know the provenance of what we are buying. I'm all for organic eating, but if the quality is not up to it, then what's the point?

You notice I mentioned mutton. Remember that? Some of us, well, most of us, have probably never experienced it, because the trend has been toward cuts that can be cooked and served quickly, with few cooking skills involved. Slow-cooked cuts such as shanks, brisket, shins, and even cheeks are where the skills lie, and these cuts need to come back into our way of eating. The good old lamb shank crops up on restaurant and gastropub menus as often as rib-eye steaks these days, and that's a sure sign that slow cooking is back.

We do need to rely on our butchers and supermarkets to offer us the various and less popular cuts, though; quite often they are guilty of not offering us enough variety, and so the poor old farmer and wholesalers end up with excess of the less popular cuts and not enough of the day to day ones. Some people get a bit confused about hanging meat and are led to believe that it tenderizes it. If an animal is stressed and tense to begin with it will not be improved by hanging; the flavour is the only thing that will improve, and that's why the provenance of the meat is important. So what about meat and wine? Rare roast beef and claret! When both are perfect, you have one of the world's great marriages, Malcolm?

A GREAT MARRIAGE? MORE LIKE A SHOTGUN WEDDING BASED ON CHEMICAL COMPULSION, MARK. The blood in the meat soothes the tannins in the wine. It's a protein interchange. Beyond doubt, killing a cow (perhaps one raised in Scotland or massaged in Japan) and crushing Cabernet Sauvignon grapes grown in a climate chilly enough to encourage firm tannins can produce a sensational union. And it is, as I say, all based on the effects of tannin, which is a vegetable extract (used commercially to cure animal hides), acting on the blood in the meat. Tannin occurs naturally in grape skins. It is an antioxidant. It protects the fruit until it is ripe.

Mark is right. Good tannic claret red wine from Bordeaux and rare meat (beef being the prime example) can lead to a fantastic marriage, because it is a wholly supportive double act; the two components are made for one another. However, who eats roast beef as we once did? Who swigs claret as we once did? Surely only

Meat, nowadays, with all the wonderful ethnic mixing of ingredients, is prepared in so many diverse ways that the old wines simply do not work.

a few old codgers, mouldering away in arcane corners of the UK, imbibe the one as they masticate the other, and all three are slowly passing into history (though claret is attempting a fighting comeback after the thrashing it has received at the hands of the Aussies, South Africans, and South Americans on the export markets). Meat, nowadays, with all the wonderful ethnic mixing of ingredients and crossover of culinary ideas and styles, is prepared in so many diverse ways that the old wines simply do not work.

Take Mark's braised pork belly – old-style red wine simply wilts (indeed new-style red wine isn't so hot either, as you will discover when you encounter the accompanying wine suggestions). Such a dish is very modern, ethnically derived from cuisines which are not native to English-speaking countries. Such cuisines have only made their stirring and imaginative presences felt over the last few decades, thanks to immigration, world travel, ethnic grocers and restaurants (and mainstream supermarkets reflecting this trend), which have caused a greater desire on many people's parts to eat more adventurously, healthily, and spicily. It is a coincidence, but a deliciously happy one, that just as this food revolution was taking place a wine revolution was explosively occurring. New World red wines, and some whites, can tackle these modern meat dishes with style and conviction. Why? Because they provide, for the most part, greater intensity of flavour, more vibrancy of fruit, and a richness which is, compared with Old World wines, not so prim, not so unwilling to go along with the mood of the drinker.

If there is anything to be learned, it is that meat by itself forms no basis for making a decision about the wine. It is the way in which the meat is cooked, and the herbs and spices it is drenched with, which are the deciding factors. Up to fifteen years ago, I would have said tell me the nationality of the chef and I will tell you which wine I will drink with his/her meat dishes. But that, as good old British chef Mark Hix demonstrates so deftly, no longer means anything. It's a wonderful new world we now live, eat, and drink in. Who'd want to go back to the old days?

Braised Pork Belly with Five Spice and Chinese Greens

SERVES 4

UNFORTUNATELY, PORK BELLY ISN'T USED MUCH THESE DAYS. I think the fat puts people off. However, the long cooking in this recipe softens and renders most of the fat away, while at the same time the pork takes on the flavours of the spices. It's a cheap cut of meat with an excellent flavour – better than some of the more expensive and more popular prime cuts.

PLAIN FLOUR, FOR DUSTING | 1KG (2LB 4OZ) PORK BELLY, BONED, RIND REMOVED, AND CUT INTO 8 X 4CM (3¼ X 1½-INCH) CHUNKS | 2TBSP SESAME OIL | 1 SMALL ONION, ROUGHLY CHOPPED | 1 MEDIUM MILD CHILLI, DESEEDED AND SLICED | 50G (1¾OZ) ROOT GINGER, PEELED AND FINELY CHOPPED | 1 STAR ANISE | 4 CLOVES GARLIC, CRUSHED | 1TSP CHINESE FIVE SPICE POWDER | 50ML (2FL OZ) LIGHT SOY SAUCE | 1.5 LITRES (2¾ PINTS) BEEF STOCK (GOOD CUBES WILL DO) | 10–15G (¼–½OZ) CORNFLOUR | 150G (5½OZ) FRESH SHIITAKE MUSHROOMS | STEAMED PAK OR BOK CHOI, TO SERVE
TO GARNISH
BUNCH OF SPRING ONIONS, TRIMMED AND SLICED ON THE ANGLE | A FEW SPRIGS OF CORIANDER

1. Lightly flour the pieces of pork belly. Heat one tablespoon of sesame oil in a heavy-based pan or flameproof casserole dish and quickly colour the pieces of pork on all sides. Add the onions, chilli, ginger, star anise, garlic, five spice, and soy.

2. Pour in the beef stock, bring to the boil, cover, and simmer gently for 2–2½ hours, skimming off the fat every so often, or until the pork is very tender. If the liquid evaporates too quickly, add a little water to stop the meat drying out.

3. Mix the cornflour with a little water and stir it into the stock to thicken it. Add the shiitake mushrooms, cover, and simmer for another 25–30 minutes. The consistency should be gravy-like. Toss the bok choi with the remaining sesame oil and serve with the pork garnished with spring onions and coriander.

CHINESE-INFLUENCED DISHES AND MIXED SPICES

Believe it or not, the first Chinatown in the UK was in Liverpool. Chinese cooks would jump ship on the Mersey and set up food stalls and cafés, and there the Chinese culture began. I'm not sure the ingredients they cooked with were as exotic as they are today. In fact, I know they weren't. The other day I bought a Chinese cookbook called *Chow,* written in the 1930s, and you would be amazed at how basic the ingredients are compared with modern day cookbooks – not a sprig of coriander or star anise in sight.

I get a lot of inspiration from wandering around Chinatown in London and my local Vietnamese supermarkets in the East End. There's always something new to buy and experiment with for the menu at the Bambou, our Vietnamese restaurant. Asian herbs and spices must be treated with respect, though, and not just thrown into anything. There is only a handful of chefs out there who really understand fusion cooking and how the spices and herbs work to the main ingredient's advantage.

BRAISED PORK BELLY WITH FIVE SPICE AND CHINESE GREENS

THIS DISH IS TOUGH ON WINE, BUT THE WINE WILL BE GENTLE ON THE POCKET. It is only necessary to find a liquid that will cleanse the palate between mouthfuls, yet at the same time enhance the flavours of the dish without overpowering them, just as the dish itself will enhance the layers of flavour in the wine. It is, therefore, essential to buy wisely but not expensively. A young Chilean Chardonnay is fine, as is Aussie, South African, and New Zealand Chardonnay (though this latter, as with Californian Chardonnay, is tending towards a price level I find unacceptable with a dish so brutally unconcerned for the niceties of complexity which many a white wine can boast but which this dish will ride roughshod over). A Sicilian Chardonnay is perfectly acceptable.

However, if I must choose one wine, from one producer, above all others, it is a *moelleux* Chenin Blanc from Domaine Huët in Vouvray in the Loire. If I had to select one grower among so many (unlike Burgundy where the outstanding specimens are so few), I would nominate Domaine Huët. This is a Biodynamic estate, now run by Noël Pinguet, a man with a bristling beard providing a thorn patch for a warm smile to break through. Through Gaston Huët, the ex-mayor of Vouvray who died in 2003 aged ninety-two, the estate has developed a reputation for extraordinary wines of longevity, finesse, and delightful (and often surprising) versatility. The wines come from three sites, all individually made and labelled as such; they are Le Haut-Lieu, Le Clos du Bourg, and Le Mont.

WINE CHECKLIST

VOUVRAY MOELLEUX OR DEMI-SEC (LOIRE – FRANCE)

CHARDONNAY (CHILE, AUSTRALIA, SOUTH AFRICA, NEW ZEALAND, CALIFORNIA, AND SICILY – ITALY)

WINE AND CHINESE-INFLUENCED DISHES
Wines which can handle Chinese dishes – Asian cuisine generally – and the mixed-spice regimes of modern so-called fusion cooking, are predominantly white. This is because such wines have a touch of fruit (perhaps sweet-edged), which works with the chillies, and acidity, which goes with the ground spices.

The Ultimate Hamburger

SERVES 4

THE WORD "HAMBURGER" NORMALLY REFERS TO PICKING UP SOME READY-MADE ONES FROM THE FREEZER DEPARTMENT, possibly the fresh section, of the high-street chains. Okay, it's quick and convenient, but what are you actually eating? If you are going to eat a lump of cooked minced beef, then why not buy some top-notch freshly minced beef and mould the hamburgers yourselves? You can then cook them rare or medium – or crucified, if you must.

800G–1KG (1LB 12OZ–2LB 4OZ) GOOD-QUALITY COARSELY MINCED BEEF, SUCH AS RIB OR RUMP, INCLUDING 30 PER CENT FAT | 40G (1½OZ) AMERICAN MUSTARD | 100G (3½OZ) TOMATO KETCHUP | 4 GOOD-QUALITY BAPS | 1 SMALL RED ONION, SLICED | 4 LARGE SWEET PICKLED GHERKINS, SLICED | 1 BEEF TOMATO, SLICED | SALT AND FRESHLY GROUND BLACK PEPPER

1. Season and mix the mince to ensure that the fat is evenly distributed throughout. Mould into four balls and shape them either with a burger press, if you have one, or by pushing the meat into a pastry cutter. The thicker, the better, so you can keep it rare, if you wish. Put the hamburgers in the refrigerator to set the meat before cooking.

2. Whisk together the American mustard and tomato ketchup for the sauce. Lightly toast the baps and keep them warm in a low oven until you have cooked the burgers.

3. The hamburgers are best cooked on a hot barbecue or griddle plate, but a smoking hot cast-iron pan will do. This seals in the juices, and will give a nicely cooked rare or medium-rare burger after a couple of minutes on each side without the juices running out. Don't cook them under the grill unless you have a red-hot American-style one, as doing so tends to boil the meat. Serve the hamburgers in the baps with slices of red onion, gherkin, and beef tomato, and the hamburger sauce.

CHUTNEYS AND PICKLES

We all take chutneys and pickles for granted, because it's easy to throw them into our shopping basket without any thought of how they got into the jars in the first place. Preserving crops up a lot in cooking, and today's equivalent is the deep-freeze. Before we had below-zero cooling, crops had to be preserved by way of pickling in the form of chutneys, jams, and pickles.

Fortunately, we have continued this form of preserving today, and crops are grown specifically for this purpose. Almost anything can be turned into a chutney with the help of sugar and vinegar. Chutneys normally consist of a mixture of ingredients and often include herbs and spices as flavouring.

The fun of making chutneys and pickles is that you can adapt and create your own bespoke recipes, especially if you grow your own vegetables and herbs. Try it and see.

THE ULTIMATE HAMBURGER

IT SEEMS TO ME THAT ON NATIONALITY AND VINOUS GROUNDS THERE IS AN OBVIOUS CHOICE OF WINE HERE: Californian Zinfandel. A vivacious specimen is required, not over-oaked or too alcoholic, and we have a choice of names. Ravenswood is good, for example, but Ridge can be better. However, may I be controversial? I'd like to offer something even wilder. To do this we must visit the Poliziano Estate in Montepulciano, Tuscany, and taste wine with Simone Tremiti. Azienda Agricola Poliziano was founded comparatively recently, 1961, but its name, Poliziano, is taken from a fifteenth-century poet, Angelo Ambrogini, who was known as, or wrote under the name of, Il Poliziano. Poliziano Rosso di Montepulciano, an 80 per cent Sangiovese (or Prugnolo Gentile, as the Montepulciano clone is called) and 20 per cent Merlot blend, can show great calm and glossy richness. Says Simone: "We use Merlot to add softness and sweetness. A 100 per cent Sangiovese is not impossible, but it would be tannic, and the wine would take years to be ready to drink." The Vino Nobile di Montepulciano (which also adds some Merlot to the predominant Prugnolo Gentile, as well as Colorino and Canaiolo Nero) is in a similar vein, but is a touch classier.

While in Tuscany, and with that hamburger awaiting a companion, let us now drop in on the village of Gaiole in Chianti to find the wine called Stielle from producer Rocca di Castagnoli. Made by Maurizio Alongi from Sangiovese and Cabernet grapes, it has real charm and depth and is a great wine to enjoy with that hamburger. However, when it came to it, it was a Sicilian Shiraz, Inycon from Planeta, which I plonked down beside the dish for the photograph, and, when the pair were consumed afterwards, there was nothing but contented sighs from the team. Which proves? That the least expensive wine is sometimes the best.

WINE CHECKLIST

ZINFANDEL (CALIFORNIA)

MONTEPULCIANO (TUSCANY – ITALY)

CHIANTI (TUSCANY – ITALY)

SHIRAZ (SICILY – ITALY)

WINE AND CHUTNEYS AND PICKLES
Chutneys and any pickles are anathema to wine because they contain dead wine already. That is to say, they contain vinegar, and this kills wines. However, with sufficient other ingredients to ride shotgun, some dishes, such as this sublime hamburger, do not ruffle red wine as otherwise they might.

Bratwurst with Rösti and Onion Sauce

SERVES 4

BRATWURST CAN BE BOUGHT FROM SOME SPECIALIST DELIS, AND YOU OCCASIONALLY SEE THEM IN SUPERMARKETS. They make a change from normal bangers, and with a good onion sauce and a crisp potato rösti they make a fun, surprise dinner-party dish. Anton Mosimann often serves them at his chef reunion dinners, and they are remarkable and hit the spot for hungry alcohol-fuelled chefs. You can lightly score the bratwurst, if you wish, which gives them a rather nice effect when grilled.

2 LARGE, FLOURY BAKING POTATOES | **1TBSP OLIVE OIL** | **4 LARGE BRATWURST SAUSAGES WEIGHING ABOUT 150G (5½OZ) EACH**
FOR THE ONION SAUCE
1TBSP VEGETABLE OIL | **2 MEDIUM ONIONS, THINLY SLICED** | **GOOD KNOB OF BUTTER** |
3TSP FLOUR | **1TSP TOMATO PURÉE** | **1TSP DIJON MUSTARD** | **100ML (3½FL OZ) RED WINE** |
250ML (9FL OZ) BEEF STOCK | **SALT AND FRESHLY GROUND BLACK PEPPER**

1. To make the sauce, heat the oil in a thick-bottomed pan and gently cook the onion for 8–10 minutes until lightly coloured. Add the butter, flour, and tomato purée, and stir well over a low heat for a minute. Add the mustard, stir well, then gradually add the red wine, stirring to avoid lumps. Slowly pour in the beef stock. Season, bring to the boil, and simmer for 20–25 minutes until the sauce has reduced by about two-thirds and thickened. If the sauce is too thick, add a little water. Remove from the heat and keep warm.

2. Meanwhile, put the whole potatoes in a pan with salted water. Cover, bring to the boil, and simmer for 20 minutes. The potatoes should be cooked two-thirds of the way through. Remove from the water and leave to cool for about 15 minutes – you can run them under cold water to speed up the process. Scrape the skin from the potatoes with a knife, and grate them on the coarse side of a grater. Put the gratings in a bowl, season, and mix well.

3. Heat a small non-stick blini pan with the oil and add a quarter of the mixture. Press the potato down lightly with a spatula and cook on a low heat for about 4–5 minutes until the bottom is lightly golden and crisp. Flip over and cook for another 4–5 minutes until crisp. Repeat with the rest of the potato, and keep them warm in a low oven. Next, to cook the sausages, grill them in a ribbed griddle pan or under a medium to hot grill for 4–5 minutes on each side until lightly coloured. Serve the bratwurst on the rösti with the sauce spooned over.

SAUSAGES

The good old banger has become a part of our national diet, and consumption must be up there with fish and chips. Sadly, sausages are regarded as cheap food, and manufacturers tend to produce them with this in mind. Sausages need a little more respect; inferior fillings with rusk, and bread extenders used to make the cost acceptable, just don't do the British banger any favours. On the upside, though, there are some great sausage-makers springing up which are filling real sausage skins with real chunky, meaty farces.

In Spain or France, you would expect to pay top money for a sausage, where chunks of meat are visible through the skins. Look at chorizo, for example; the process is not a simple one and the pigs, more often than not, are specially reared – much like the Pata Negra hams. The sausage is an interesting food, because across the world it has different values depending on its style and the process it goes through.

BRATWURST WITH ROSTI AND ONION SAUCE

TREAD CAREFULLY, DEAR WINE WAITER. What seems a fairly robust dish is, in fact, more delicate than you would suppose. It requires, in spite of the caramelization of the onions, a wine of matching delicacy (which is not to say it will lack emphasis or character). How does a German Riesling with Spätlese level of ripeness sound? Grotesque? Shame on you. Such a wine is required, not solely on grounds of nationality compatibility, but also on those of the levels of richness in dish and glass complementing and enhancing one another. There is an alternative; but it is also German. A Pinot Gris from the Pfalz (Villa Wolf) is a useful one to have with this dish, but much more widely available are, of course, those Spätlesen; let me reel off these names: Loosen (Mosel), Anheuser (Nahe), J.J. Prüm (Mosel), Robert Weil (Rheingau), Willi Haag, Muller-Catoir, and at least forty others.

Why such white wine when most people think red wine is a sausage's natural partner? Because the richness of this dish needs the cutting acidity of Riesling along with the Spätlese level of ripeness (or sweetness). German wine is bedevilled (or graced, depending on your point of view) by a system that classifies wines by the level of ripeness at time of picking, no matter what happens in the winery to create a dry or an off-dry style from super-ripe grapes. It is one of those maddening characteristics of German wine, which to some is eminently logical and rational, but to the rest is, at times, bordering on the insane.

WINE CHECKLIST

RIESLING SPATLESE (ALL GERMAN REGIONS)

PINOT GRIS (PFALZ – GERMANY)

WINE AND SAUSAGES

Bratwurst, along with certain other German sauages, benefit from being paired with a white wine, but most other sauages (like, say, the garlicky French Toulouse or the rustic Italian cotechino) get along better with red wines. A sausage, where wine is concerned, is not just a sausage.

Cassoulet de Toulouse

SERVES 4

THIS IS A RENOWNED DISH FROM THE SOUTHWEST, BUT SERVED THROUGHOUT FRANCE WITH VARIOUS INGREDIENTS, normally containing duck or goose, smoked pork, mutton in some cases, and, in Toulouse especially, Toulouse sausage. This is a slightly simplified version, but you can easily adapt it. It's important to use good-quality dried beans that haven't been hanging around in the cupboard for years as those will take for ever to cook. I've given the weight for canned beans; if you are using dried beans, soak overnight, and cook according to the instructions until tender. The duck or goose fat, and the duck or goose confit, can also come from a can or jar.

2–3TBSP **DUCK FAT** | 1 MEDIUM ONION, FINELY CHOPPED | 4 CLOVES GARLIC, CRUSHED | 1TSP CHOPPED FRESH THYME LEAVES | ½TBSP FLOUR | 1TSP TOMATO PUREE | 100ML (3½FL OZ) WHITE WINE | ½ LITRE (18FL OZ) HOT BEEF STOCK | 4 X 100G (3½OZ) CHUNKS OF SMOKED OR UNSMOKED STREAKY BACON OR PANCETTA | 4 CONFIT DUCK LEGS OR 2 CONFIT GOOSE LEGS, CUT IN HALF AT THE JOINT | 4 SMALL TOULOUSE SAUSAGES, EACH WEIGHING ABOUT 60G (2¼OZ) | 250G (9OZ) COOKED, SMALL HARICOT BEANS | 80G (2¾OZ) FRESH WHITE BREADCRUMBS | SALT AND FRESHLY GROUND BLACK PEPPER

1. Preheat the oven to 200ºC/400ºF/Gas mark 6. In a heavy-bottomed ovenproof pan, gently heat the duck fat, and cook the onion, garlic, and thyme for 4–5 minutes until soft and lightly coloured. Add the flour and stir well for a couple of minutes until it begins to colour. Add the tomato purée and stir, then gradually stir in the wine and hot stock.

2. Bring to the boil and add the pieces of bacon. Cover with a lid and simmer gently for 1 hour, or until tender. Meanwhile, roast the duck legs and sausages in the oven for 15–20 minutes until lightly coloured. Remove and turn the oven down to 170ºC/325ºF/Gas mark 3.

3. Add the sausages, beans, and duck to the pan, mix together gently, and cook in the oven for 1 hour. Scatter the crumbs on top and cook in the oven for another 15 minutes – this will soak up the excess fat and give a nice finish to the dish. The pork provides salt, so don't add any until you've checked the seasoning before you serve.

MIXING MEAT, POULTRY, AND GAME
Combining meats in dishes is common all over the world. I could reel off a long list of dishes, from the famous Cassoulet de Toulouse to the Liverpool lobscouse. They all have their regional variations, depending on what is available at the time and how much the pocket can stretch to. The good old paella, for example, can consist of what was gathered and hunted that day, whether on land or sea, and what's in season. The idea of mixing up different meats, poultry, and game with perhaps root vegetables or native pulses dates back many centuries, and to this day, here and abroad, these dishes are still getting cooked up by peasants and gourmets to make hearty feasts for work and play.

CASSOULET DE TOULOUSE

THIS LEGENDARY DISH, IT WAS CLAIMED IN THE BRITAIN OF THE 1960s, ONLY EXISTED IN THE LANGUEDOC (in several regional variants), and so, in order to experience *le vrai cassoulet*, a small journey was necessary. It took five days to drive from Calais, via Burgundy, to Cahors, to finally fetch up (and the expression is finely chosen) at Chez Paulette – then renowned for the pertinacity of its cassoulet. We had a whole copper pot of cassoulet to ourselves. Over four hours we demolished it and then, over the next six days, the dish proceeded to demolish me. It took me six days to recover from Paulette's cassoulet. Had I swallowed a bag of cement? A recalcitrant boulder was lodged in my midriff and no amount of the local red wine, however copious, shifted the feeling of fullness for a week.

Let me tell you, Mark's cassoulet is a model of digestive finesse and deliciousness in comparison, but even so this is not a light dish. It is, I feel, best tackled at lunch, so you can have a siesta afterward and drink nothing but water (all right then, a glass of white wine) and eat little but a salad for dinner. It is a dish of rustic richness, however much its more rugged (or should I say jagged?) edges are smoothed by chefs such as Mr Hix, and red wine is demanded.

Aussie Shirazes and Cabernets suit it admirably, for they contain the perfect degree of sunshine and flowers, herbs and fruit, to meld with both the meat and the rich stock and beans (Dalwhinnie Moonambel Shiraz is a truly luxurious accompaniment to this dish). Interestingly, the wine I drank with my inauguration cassoulet, Cahors *naturellement*, is okay, but not as palate-enhancing as one or two Aussie Merlots (one of which is Deakin Estate Merlot which from the 2002 vintage has come in a screwcap to keep its sumptuous tannins frisky). Château du Cèdre makes a tannically assertive Cahors in France which when decanted for twelve hours becomes toothsome and comely without losing its character or bite.

WINE CHECKLIST

SHIRAZ (AUSTRALIA)

CABERNET SAUVIGNON (AUSTRALIA)

MERLOT (AUSTRALIA)

CAHORS (FRANCE)

WINE AND MIXED-MEAT DISHES
It is fair to say that dishes which mix meats, game, and poultry (and may include sausages) do require hearty reds, but not those with so much heartiness they clog the throat. An over-alcoholic Aussie Shiraz, then (say over 14.5 degrees of alcohol), is overdoing it. In some instances, a Beaujolais-style red, fresh and extremely perky, is to be preferred.

Steak Tartare

SERVES 4

YOU RARELY SEE THIS DISH ON RESTAURANT MENUS AS IT'S TRADITIONALLY MIXED AT THE TABLE, WHICH IS SOMETHING OF A DYING ART. Get your butcher to mince it fresh, or use a mincer attachment, if you have one on your machine. Otherwise, chop it finely by hand with a heavy knife.

500G (1LB 2OZ) VERY FRESH, LEAN FILLET OF SIRLOIN OR TOPSIDE STEAK, MINCED | 3 SHALLOTS, FINELY CHOPPED | 2TBSP CAPERS | | 2TBSP GHERKINS, CHOPPED | A FEW DASHES OF BRANDY | ½TBSP TOMATO KETCHUP | 1 EGG YOLK | 2–3TSP WORCESTERSHIRE SAUCE, TO TASTE | A FEW DASHES OF TABASCO | 1TBSP OLIVE OIL | SALT AND FRESHLY GROUND BLACK PEPPER

1. Mix all the ingredients together and check the seasoning – you may wish to add a little more Tabasco, ketchup or Worcestershire sauce.

2. Spoon the steak tartare onto a plate, or, if you prefer, push it into a ramekin or mould and turn out onto a plate to serve. Serve with fine-cut chips, green salad or toast.

HOT, SPICY DISHES

The fear of spice is normally due to a bad or surprise experience. Children and grown-ups who have had a conservative culinary upbringing are generally the shyest when it comes to a little heat in their food. When I moved to London from the West Country, I went straight into it and got a real craving for Indian, Mexican, and whatever other fiery solids I could get down my neck. Cold beer during and before always helped the cause, although I'm not so daring now and would rather taste the spices than the heat. A trip to New Orleans a couple years ago, to McIlhenny's on Avery Island, certainly brushed up my knowledge on the fiery Tabasco – and whiskey sours, of course.

STEAK TARTARE

MANY A DISH IS A MINEFIELD. That is to say, the wine waiter must tread warily lest the proffered wine is not to die a death once it clashes with the dish's hidden, spicy ingredients. But Mark's steak tartare is considerably more belligerent than a mere minefield. Capers and gherkins are explosive enough, but Tabasco? Worcestershire sauce? Brandy? The wine waiter who knows his onions (or, in this case, shallots) tiptoes quietly from the fray and resigns, muttering "I surrender!" as he does so. But this option is not open to me. Mark has brought the dish to table. I must descend to the cellar and emerge with a suitable bottle.

My heart says Cabernet Sauvignon (with the tannins to handle the raw beef), but my head says Shiraz (to put up a fight against those flavourings). The only answer, in such a fix, is to turn to the Cape and its unique Pinotage grape. This is almost exclusively a South African growth, though I did taste the last bottle of a Californian Pinotage before phylloxera devastated the vineyard and it was grubbed up. It must be a young Pinotage, what's more, within a year of its vintage release, if possible. With such youth the tannins are still buttressed by sweet, slightly spicy fruit, with that characteristic, burned-rubber undertone of the grape, and it is this we need to counteract the steak's inflammable components. Names to look for are Clos Malverne and Kanonkop,

There is an Aussie red which can cope with this dish: Mount Ida Heathcote Shiraz from a lovely corner of Victoria. But hold on. There's a white wine in the picture. Ah yes. It occured to me, as Jason the photographer fussed around the set getting the various bits and pieces of the dish to look great on that slab of wood, that some people prefer white wine with this dish. If so, I unhestitatingly select one from the Casa Lapostolle Estate in Chile, from its Cuvée Alexandre range.

WINE AND HOT, SPICY DISHES
Steak tartare is surely one of the oddest dishes in the world. This is because it is such an incredible sum of its various parts that any deviance from the precise ingredients, in the exact, specified quantities, produces another dish altogether (and therefore the recommended wine will falter). So be warned. If the dish is spicy, a more robust wine is needed. Tabasco used to excess is no friend of wine.

WINE CHECKLIST

PINOTAGE (SOUTH AFRICA)

SHIRAZ (VICTORIA – AUSTRALIA)

CHARDONNAY (CHILE)

Lamb Baked in Hay with Lavender

SERVES 4–6

COOKING WITH HAY IS AN OLD METHOD, ALMOST LIKE THE FRENCH EN PAPILLOTE. The hay keeps the heat in and gives the meat a grassy taste. But it's important to soak the hay for 15 minutes before using – if it smoulders it will give the lamb an undesirable taste. This method works well in Agas, where you can lose heat if different things are cooking in the oven and the door is being opened and closed. Pet shops and garden centres sell clean hay.

2 X 8-BONE FRENCH-TRIMMED RACK OF LAMB | SALT AND FRESHLY GROUND BLACK PEPPER | A LITTLE VEGETABLE OIL | 1 HEAD OF NEW-SEASON GARLIC, OR A FEW CLOVES OF NORMAL GARLIC, THINLY SLICED | A FEW SPRIGS OF LAVENDER | A COUPLE OF GOOD HANDFULS OF CLEAN HAY, SOAKED IN WATER AND DRAINED

1. Preheat the oven to 220°C/425°F/ Gas mark 7. Season the lamb, then heat a little oil until it's almost smoking in a heavy frying pan that fits the lamb. Seal the lamb on all sides until nicely browned, then remove. Make 9 or 10 incisions about 1cm (half an inch) deep through the skin, and insert a slice of garlic and a sprig of lavender in each. If using new-season garlic, you only need to peel the outer skin.

2. Put the lamb into a roasting tray and pack the hay around it. Cover with foil and cook in the oven for 20 minutes. Remove the foil and turn the oven down to 190°C/375°F/Gas mark 5. Cook for another 15 minutes for medium rare.

3. Leave to rest for 15 minutes, then remove the hay and carve. If you leave it in the hay any longer, it will continue cooking to medium. Serve with the first of the new-season Jersey royals roasted in a little olive oil. Feed the hay to pet rabbits, or put it round the strawberry plants.

FLORAL HERBS

The use of flowers is not uncommon in cooking, although some of the food trends in the eighties did abuse them and some cooks now frown upon their place in the kitchen. There are many decorative herbs we cultivate and grow in our gardens that easily find their way into our kitchens, such as rosemary, lavender, and nasturtiums.

Nasturtiums are rather peppery, and their flavour could easily be passed off for watercress or land cress. Their flowers are equally tasty in salads, and it's a useful way to keep them trimmed by adding them to the salad bowl.

Elderflowers are one of my favourites though, especially for flavouring jellies or cordials, or dipping in a light batter to be fried and served alongside elderflower ice-cream.

At the end of last summer, when my herbs were flowering, I made some savoury jellies with thyme and rosemary flowers by adding them to apple juice. They made a great alternative to the normal lamb accompaniments.

LAMB BAKED IN HAY WITH LAVENDER

A SENSUAL WINE IS REQUIRED HERE: a wine of a delicate richness similar to that of the dish; one as classy, aromatic, loving. Surely, then, only a Pinot Noir will suffice? One says Pinot, and burgundies spring to mind. This means specific producers, and with this lamb I offer three candidates: Engel, Leroy, and Dujac.

New Zealand Pinots can also be exceptional, and those from Central Otago, with its cool, oft-times chill climate, offer exciting fruits. Names to look for are Chard Farm, Rippon, Mount Difficulty, and Peregrine. Villa Maria, Cloudy Bay, Jackson Estate, and Wither Hills in Marlborough can also be excellent. If you can find it (and it is worth the hunt) Neudorf Pinot Noir from Tim and Judy Finn in Nelson can be New Zealand's most compelling Pinot. It is also the perfect liquid accompaniment if you cook lamb in the traditional way, with rosemary (and perhaps garlic). Pinot Noir loves rosemary and adores lamb.

But do not overlook Austria. Pittenauer has turned out some exciting Pinots, uniting the sexiness of wild-strawberry-drenched satin with the fragrant intensity of truffles. However, where else can we turn for Pinots which have at least a hint of this excitement? Increasingly, Chilean Pinots emerge with credibility and consistency. Concha y Toro's Casillero del Diablo, Cono Sur, and Montes Casablanca Valley all offer varying degrees of cassis and cherry crunchiness with deft tannins.

There is also South Africa to consider, and Hamilton Russell, along with Bouchard Finlayson's Tête du Cuvée Galpin Peak, is outstanding (the latter, in some vintages, the most complete Pinot I've tasted from the Cape).

Lastly, there is California. With this dish, I suggest either La Crema or Marimar Torres. Both bring to the feast that gamy richness which makes Pinot so perfect with this dish.

WINE CHECKLIST

PINOT NOIR (BURGUNDY, NEW ZEALAND, AUSTRIA, CHILE, SOUTH AFRICA, AND CALIFORNIA)

WINE AND FLORAL HERBS

Herbs with a floral perfume and flavour are tricky components for wine to accompany. They need to be gingerly considered. For never forget that it is not the herb by itself which knocks against the wine but its effect on the main ingredient, which in the case of meat must mean matching red wines with perfume and gaminess.

Grilled Veal Chop with Treviso and Italian Onions

SERVES 4

VEAL CHOPS OR CUTLETS ARE A GREAT CUT OF MEAT TO COOK AT HOME. They are normally taken from the rib, a moister cut because of its higher fat content, or from the loin. Italian onions or cipolline are similar to button onions but flatter in shape, and can occasionally be bought fresh or in jars as antipasti. Treviso, or trevisiano, is a member of the radicchio and endive family, and looks a bit like a long red chicory. It can be bought from good greengrocers. Otherwise, radicchio will work equally well.

16–20 MEDIUM-SIZED CIPOLLINE, RAW OR COOKED | 4–5TBSP OLIVE OIL | SALT AND FRESHLY GROUND BLACK PEPPER | 2 HEADS OF TREVISO | 4 VEAL CHOPS, WEIGHING ABOUT 250G (9OZ) EACH | 1TSP CHOPPED FRESH THYME OR OREGANO LEAVES | 1TBSP BALSAMIC VINEGAR

1. If you are using fresh cipolline, cook them in a covered ovenproof dish in a moderate oven, with a tablespoon of olive oil and seasoning, for 35–40 minutes, stirring every so often until tender. Cover with foil if they are over-browning.

Quarter the treviso, remove the root, and separate the leaves.

2. Preheat a griddle pan or grill. Season and lightly oil the chops. Grill for 4–5 minutes on each side until just pink. Meanwhile, heat 2 tablespoons of olive oil in a large frying pan, add the treviso leaves and thyme, season, and cook on a low heat for 4–5 minutes, stirring, until the leaves soften. Add a little water if the leaves begin to colour.

3. Add the onions and continue to cook for another 4–5 minutes on a low heat. Pour in the balsamic vinegar, stir well, and remove from the heat.

Spoon the treviso and onions onto warmed serving plates, lay the chops on top, and spoon any juices around.

VEAL

It's a shame people find veal so tricky to get hold of. It seems that the only place to get it is in good restaurants, especially Italian ones. A good butcher, if you are lucky to have one nearby, should stock veal, but generally it's one of those scary meats that people just don't want to buy or cook. Baby cow – why not? We eat lots of other baby animals. Oh well, it is a shame, because it is so tasty, especially the offal. It's difficult to turn down a dish of calves' liver and bacon.

GRILLED VEAL CHOP WITH TREVISO AND ITALIAN ONIONS

OH, HOW SPLENDIDLY MCLAREN VALE SHIRAZ GOES WITH THIS DISH, along with Cabernet Sauvignon or Cabernet/Merlot from Hawke's Bay in New Zealand's North Island. These wines are not difficult to find. However, a rarer, and arguably more perfect, choice of wine – a wine which doesn't even feature in our photograph of candidate bottles – is one of two from the Tenuta di Ghizzano Estate, run by Ginevra Venerosi Pesciolini (who can trace the estate's roots back to 1370). The wines are of the humble Colline Pisane denomination, and the two I offer you are Veneroso Tenuta di Ghizzano, a Cabernet/Sangiovese blend, and Nambrot Tenuta di Ghizzano, a Merlot/Cabernet Sauvignon/Petit Verdot marriage.

"The St-Emilion of Tuscany," jokes Ginevra, pouring me the last named. "What an insult to a greater wine than most St-Emilions can ever be," I whisper. Just regard the colour! Feel the sensuality of the texture! Experience the sheer excitement of the complex berries and those svelte yet characterful tannins! St-Emilion? When did you last find coffee and chocolate in a St-Emilion?

WINE CHECKLIST

SHIRAZ (MCLAREN VALE – AUSTRALIA)

CABERNET SAUVIGNON (HAWKE'S BAY – NEW ZEALAND)

CABERNET/MERLOT BLEND (HAWKE'S BAY – NEW ZEALAND)

CABERNET BLENDS (TUSCANY – ITALY)

Steak, Oyster, and Guinness Pie

SERVES 4–6

OYSTERS WERE ONCE CHEAP AND PLENTIFUL; they would replace the kidneys or bulk up the meat content of the pie to give the gravy a slight taste of the Irish Sea. Serve this with plain mashed potatoes, or add some chopped cooked cabbage and spring onions to the mash to make colcannon.

800G (1LB 12OZ) BRAISING BEEF, PREFERABLY FLANK, SKIRT OR SHIN, CUT INTO ROUGH 3CM (1¼-INCH) CUBES | GLASS OF RED WINE | 150ML (5FL OZ) GUINNESS | 1TSP CHOPPED THYME LEAVES | 1 BAY LEAF | VEGETABLE OIL, FOR FRYING | 2TBSP PLAIN FLOUR, PLUS EXTRA FOR FLOURING | SALT AND FRESHLY GROUND BLACK PEPPER | GOOD KNOB OF BUTTER | 1 MEDIUM ONION, FINELY CHOPPED | 1TSP TOMATO PURÉE | 1.5 LITRES (2¾ PINTS) BEEF STOCK | ABOUT 1TSP CORNFLOUR (OPTIONAL) | 350–400G (12–14OZ) GOOD-QUALITY PUFF PASTRY | 1 EGG, BEATEN | 4 LARGE ROCK OYSTERS, OR MORE IF YOU WISH, SHUCKED

1. Two days ahead, put the pieces of beef into a non-reactive bowl with the wine, Guinness, thyme, and bay leaf. Cover with clingfilm and marinate in the refrigerator for 24 hours.

Drain the meat in a colander, reserving the marinade, and dry on some kitchen paper. Heat the oil in a heavy frying pan, lightly flour the meat with half a tablespoon of the flour, seasoned with salt and pepper, and fry the meat in batches, over a high heat, until nicely browned.

2. Heat the butter in a large pan, and gently fry the onion for a few minutes until soft. Add the remaining flour and tomato purée, and stir over a low heat for a minute. Slowly add the marinade, stirring constantly to avoid lumps forming. Bring to the boil and simmer until it has reduced by half. Add the stock and the pieces of beef, bring back to the boil, cover, and simmer gently for 2 hours, until the meat is tender. It may need an extra half an hour, depending on the cut. The sauce should have thickened to a gravy-like consistency. If not, mix a little cornflour to a paste with some water, stir into the sauce, and simmer for a few minutes. Leave to cool and use to fill four individual pie dishes, or one large one, to about 1cm (½ inch) from the top.

3. Roll the puff pastry out on a floured surface to a thickness of about 5mm (¼ inch) and cut out tops for the pie dishes about 2cm (¾ inch) larger all the way round. Brush the edges of the dishes with beaten egg. Place the shucked oysters on top of the pie filling and lay the pastry on top, pressing the sides down. Cut a small slit in the top and brush all over with beaten egg. Leave to rest in a cool place for 30 minutes. Preheat the oven to 200°C/400°F/Gas mark 6, and cook the pies for 40–50 minutes, until the pastry is golden.

OFFAL

I often get asked about my favourite food, and my usual reply is offal. A lot of people hate it, but have never tried it.

Some will love pâté and not entertain the idea of liver. For me, all offal, whether it be chitterlings, tripe or sweetbreads, is just wonderful and totally underused. Okay, it is not the easiest thing to sell on a restaurant menu, but at home it can be cooked in all sorts of delicious ways.

I once had some rognons blancs (veal testicles) in the freezer and made them into Moroccan spiced cigars for my girls' christening. They went down a treat. Naturally, no one believed me when I announced what they were!

STEAK, OYSTER, AND GUINNESS PIE

THIS IS ONE OF THOSE TRADITIONAL DISHES WHICH MANY PEOPLE SWEAR CAN ONLY BE EATEN ACCOMPANIED BY BLACK STOUT, usually a Guinness. I am not fond of beer and food. Beer is fine with nuts, outside a pub on a torrid summer afternoon, but it is indigestible and filling when matched with food (and it is certainly to be avoided with Indian, Bangladeshi, and Pakistani food). So, without this avenue to explore, what are we left with? The purist would insist on one kind of wine for beef (a red) and another (white) for oysters. This dilemma inevitably invited the suggestion that a rosé is the answer, but I am not fond of this style of wine with this dish except in one instance: Cabernet Sauvignon Rosé from Chile or Hungary.

But, in a way, a rosé, though perfectly charming company with this dish, is also a compromise. Do we not want rigorous, untrammelled, 100 per cent perfection? A wine with chutzpah, style, wit, oodles of fruit, yet masses of finesse (if finesse can be exhibited massly)? The answer has to be yes, and therefore allow me to pour for you a glass of Montes Alpha Cabernet Sauvignon from Chile.

Note that ideally the wine should be permitted 3 to 4 hours of breathing beforehand to expand its acidity, concentrate its tannins, and ingnite its fruit more fully. This can be done by pouring it into a glass jug or decanter (though these are often so pretentious in design they are to be shunned). This gives the wine greater polish, yet does not mar its character (and this is a characterful wine). Isn't it delicious? Some hedonists might aver it is merely, this wine, an excuse to prepare this pie. I wouldn't argue.

WINE CHECKLIST

CABERNET SAUVIGNON ROSE (CHILE AND HUNGARY)

CABERNET SAUVIGNON (CHILE)

4
Poultry and Game

GAME CAN BE A FINE THING. THE ONLY PROBLEM IS BUYING THE STUFF. High street retailers, with a few exceptions, are a bit conservative, because most customers just don't know what to do with game once they get it home. The rules for game birds are similar to those for poultry, but, generally, less cooking time is needed as game birds vary in size. The preferred way is to keep feathered and furred game pink, unless you are braising, as otherwise you may well be wasting your time and money. Try to buy fresh game; you risk losing all the blood on defrosting frozen game.

> The rules for game birds are similar to those for poultry, but, generally, less cooking time is needed.

For the last couple of years I have been using Goosnargh poultry, which is produced by Reg Johnson in Lancashire. A lot of customers' first reactions were that the birds were a bit skinny, but before long they were quite convinced that it was the best chicken they'd eaten. Chickens shouldn't be plump and taste of nothing. They should have a natural shape and taste almost like a guinea fowl, which is what a lot of our customers commented on. So next time you buy a chicken, don't go for the fattest but for the ones that look natural; they taste the best.

POULTRY COOKING TIMES
For a 1–1.5kg (2lb 4oz–3lb 5oz) bird, allow about 1¼ hours in a fairly hot oven at 200°C/400°F/Gas mark 6.

For a 4.5–5.5kg (10–12lb) turkey, allow 30 minutes per kg (15 minutes per pound) at 190°C/375°F/Gas mark 5.

GAME SEASONS AND COOKING TIMES
Grouse (August 12 to December 10)
Rub the breasts with a little butter and roast on a high heat, 220°C/425°F/Gas mark 7, for 15 minutes for pink.

Snipe (August 12 to January 31)
Cook as for grouse.

Partridge (September 1 to February 1)
Cook as for grouse.

Mallard (September 1 to February 20)
Cook as for grouse, but for 30 minutes.

Widgeon (September 1 to February 20)
Cook as for grouse, but for 15–20 minutes.

Pheasant (October 1 to February 1)
Rub the breasts with butter, cover with streaky bacon or sliced pork fat, and cook for 25 minutes at 200°C/400°F/Gas mark 6.

Venison (season varies according to species and place)
Cooking varies according to cut and size.

Wild rabbit (all year round)
Braise legs and remove fillets to fry until pink for use in salads.

Wood pigeon (all year round)
Cook as for grouse.

ALMOST INVARIABLY, RED WINE IS SERVED WITH POULTRY AND GAME DISHES. Many times, though, this is an ill-advised course. With a roast duck and cherry sauce in an Alsatian restaurant I once enjoyed a peachy Tokay Pinot Gris poured into my glass by its maker. It was superb. I was once offered a Rhine Riesling to accompany a chicken in tarragon cream. It was magnificent. What these couplings of food and wine reveal is that it is wise to consider the pungency of the accompanying sauce when deciding what wine is appropriate. To be sure, a rare duck breast, unadorned, suits a rich red just as a chicken in the style of a coq au vin demands the kind of red wine in which the fowl was stewed.

Another way to proceed, however, is to choose the wine first, and then decide what is best to eat with it. See the label in the photograph? It is seventy-five per cent of a proud Piedmontese name, Gaja (Sori San Lorenzo is the vineyard). Only a few times in

my life have I been fortunate enough to sample fully mature specimens from this astonishing estate outside the tasting room. It can always be said of a wine – a handy stick with which to beat wine critics, this – that it was never designed to be gargled with and spat into a bucket at a tasting; and, along with a few other truly great wines on this planet, the Barbarescos of Angelo Gaja are so well suited to poultry and game dishes that the professional taster must take this into account when assessing them in the clinical, and foodless, arena of the tasting room.

To taste such a wine is an experience; to dine with such a wine is to eat with a Rita Hayworth who has the mind of a Leonardo da Vinci (for further celebrity extravagancies, please see the recipe for braised goose). True, this book is about putting wines to dishes, but just for a moment let us imagine we have a bottle of Gaja Barbaresco... and so what do we eat? A roast chicken with forty-eight cloves of garlic is a great idea. Grouse or pheasant is even better. Venison? Why, of course.

I suppose what am I hinting at here is a reversal of the way this book was researched and compiled. Mark's dishes rule the roost here, but what if I were given the scope to choose 100 great wines, appended to which were the best dishes to eat with them? "The Dishes to Eat with the World's Top 100 Wines." Gaja would feature strongly in such a book, as would so many dishes of the poultry and game repertoire.

To taste such a wine is an experience; to dine with such a wine is to eat with a Rita Hayworth who has the mind of a Leonardo da Vinci (for further celebrity extravagancies, please see the recipe for braised goose).

(Mark:) I can see where you're coming from, Malcolm. You want the wine cellar to call the shots, not the kitchen. Dream on!

Venison Escalope with Chestnuts and Chanterelles

SERVES 4

VENISON CAN BE A TRICKY AND AN EXPENSIVE CUT OF MEAT TO SERVE IF YOU DON'T KNOW WHAT YOU ARE DOING. This cut can be taken from the inner, tender muscle of the leg, the rump, or the fillets under the saddle. You will need to get your butcher's advice, depending on what he has got. It's always good to know the provenance as venison is a general word for red deer, fallow deer, and roe deer. The flavour of venison, like beef, can vary tremendously depending on age, cut, and hanging. Venison should be hung for some time to improve the flavour, otherwise freshly shot venison can end up tasting just like beef.

The other alternative is to marinate the venison in a mixture of red wine, oil, herbs, and juniper berries. This works well for cuts that are going to be cooked for longer periods, but if they've been hung they will need no marinating. If you do like the flavour, then marinate the fillets overnight or for twenty-four hours maximum, before batting them out into escalopes.

20 FRESH OR PRE-PACKED CHESTNUTS | 80G (3OZ) BUTTER | 150G (5½OZ) CHANTERELLES OR OTHER WILD MUSHROOM | SALT AND FRESHLY GROUND BLACK PEPPER | 1TBSP CHOPPED PARSLEY | 4 VENISON ESCALOPES, EACH WEIGHING ABOUT 140–150G (5–5½OZ) AND BATTED TO ABOUT ½CM (¼INCH) | 1TBSP VEGETABLE OIL

1. If you are using fresh chestnuts, preheat the oven to 200°C/400°F/Gas mark 6. Make an incision in the pointed end of each nut with a sharp knife, and roast them on a tray for 15 minutes. Remove from the oven and leave to cool. Carefully peel the nuts, removing as much of the brown skin as possible, and halve them.

2. Heat the butter in a frying pan, and cook the chestnuts for 2–3 minutes on a low heat. Add the chanterelles, season, and stir on a medium heat for 2 minutes. Add the parsley, and remove from the heat.

3. Meanwhile, season the venison. Heat a large frying pan with the oil until almost smoking and cook the escalopes for 1 minute on each side (you might need to do this in two batches).

Transfer the venison to warmed plates and spoon the chanterelles and chestnuts over.

WILD MUSHROOMS

I am a bit of a hunter-gatherer, and have been gathering fungi for years. Not only is it good exercise, but it's fun and doesn't cost you anything. Well, that's not entirely true these days, because you need a licence in many forests to pick mushrooms. We are not a nation of mushroom-pickers; most of the people I bump into in the woods are Italian or Polish. We have as many species as most here, and recently I have come across two people I know who have found truffles. In fact, one of them has owned a truffle dog for a couple years, and he has only just come up trumps. Sh, I can't say any more on that subject, I'm afraid.

The strange thing with mushrooms is that they are unpredictable. I have visited the same spot for three years after a successful harvest of trompettes de la mort and found nothing. The moon and weather conditions play a big part in the mystery of mushrooms.

Just last year, I had a tip-off about a full moon, and off we set, baskets in hand. It was one of the most successful hauls of chanterelles ever; we had to stop for legal reasons – don't like breaking the law.

VENISON ESCALOPE WITH CHESTNUTS AND CHANTERELLES

WHEN I TASTED THIS DEEPLY SAVOURY DISH, Mark inviting me to dig in the moment the venison hit the plate, a flurry of assertive red wines made their generous presences felt in my brain (a wine writer, note, is one of those rare, perhaps unique, individuals, who can become a mite tiddly just thinking about a wine long before it has ever reached the glass). First up was Mas La Plana, the great Cabernet Sauvignon from Miguel Torres in Catalonia. This wine has a pungently luxurious feel, exactly like Mark's dish.

Then, the reds of Toro come to mind. This region, overshadowed by Ribero del Duero and Rueda, grows a variety of Tempranillo called Tinto de Toro, but the style is soft and more accommodating than those of its neighbours (and often funkier than Rioja). Names to look for are Toro Farina, the Maruve label from Frutos Villar, the Cermeno label from co-op Vino de Toro. Staying in Spain, I then found Priorato jostling for recognition in the sturdy forms of Mas Martinet, Masia Duch, and Masia Barril. Tarragona is the region, Garnacha the main grape. Lastly from Spain, we have to include in this litany any red (from the Tempranillo grape) made by Albet i Noya. And then back to the Languedoc, to the brilliant screwcapped reds of Edouard Labeye. His Grenache/Syrah, Cuvée Gauthier Carignan, and Cuvée Guilhem Syrah are superb and, with this dish, gobsmackingly toothsome. Springfield Estate Cabernet Sauvignon from the Cape is also a wine to consider here.

WINE CHECKLIST

CABERNET SAUVIGNON (CATALONIA – SPAIN, SOUTH AFRICA)

TORO RED (SPAIN)

PRIORAT RED (CATALONIA – SPAIN)

GRENACHE/SYRAH BLEND (LANGUEDOC – FRANCE)

WINE AND WILD MUSHROOMS
Wild mushrooms, if they are the dominant ingredient in a dish, demand a wild, perhaps funky, wine – that is to say gamey. All the wines recommended will work, but one will work best of all (if the mushrooms are very wild and by themselves). This is Torres Mas La Plana.

Braised Goose in Red Wine

SERVES 4-6

GOOSE CAN BE JUST AS BAD AS TURKEY WHEN INCORRECTLY ROASTED, as the breast, like a turkey's, can dry out before the legs are cooked. By braising the goose you can avoid any tough or dry cuts. Another advantage is that, unlike a roast, you can cook it up to three or four days in advance and reheat on the day.

1 GOOD QUALITY GOOSE, WEIGHING 3-3.5KG (6LB 8OZ-7LB 10OZ) | **SALT AND FRESHLY GROUND BLACK PEPPER**
FOR THE SAUCE
8 LARGE SHALLOTS, FINELY CHOPPED | **2 CLOVES GARLIC, CRUSHED** | **100G (3½OZ) BUTTER** | **5TBSP FLOUR** | **1TBSP TOMATO PURÉE** | **750ML RED WINE** | **2 LITRES (3½ PINTS) HOT CHICKEN STOCK** | **A FEW SPRIGS OF THYME** | **1 BAY LEAF**

1. Preheat the oven to 220°C/425°F/Gas mark 7. With a heavy chopping knife, cut the goose in half (or get your butcher to do it). Cut off the parson's nose, and trim away any excess fat and the backbone where there is no meat. Remove the legs and cut them in half. Cut each half-breast into four pieces. Season the pieces, then roast them for 30–40 minutes, until nicely browned, turning them occasionally and draining off any fat into a bowl. (Keep this for roast potatoes or confit.)

2. Meanwhile, gently cook the shallots and garlic in the butter for 2–3 minutes until soft and lightly coloured. Add the flour and stir well over a low heat for a minute. Add the tomato purée, and gradually pour in the wine, stirring well to avoid any lumps, then stir in the hot stock. Bring to the boil, add the herbs, and simmer for 15 minutes. Remove the goose from the oven and drain in a colander over a bowl to reserve the fat.

Turn the oven to 170°C/325°F/Gas mark 3. Put the goose into a casserole dish with the sauce, cover, and braise for 2 hours or until tender.

3. Remove the pieces of goose from the liquid, put them on a plate, and cover with foil. Transfer the cooking liquid to a large saucepan, skim off any fat with a ladle, and simmer until the sauce has thickened. Return the pieces of goose to the sauce and season with salt and pepper, if necessary. At this point you can keep the dish in the fridge for a few days. To serve, bring back to the boil and simmer for 4–5 minutes. Arrange the goose on plates or a serving dish and spoon over the sauce.

Serve with the creamed polenta (*see* recipe below).

CREAMED POLENTA
Serves 4
Bring 750ml (1¼ pints) of milk to the boil in a thick-bottomed pan. Add 1 crushed garlic clove, 1 bay leaf, salt and pepper, and a pinch of nutmeg.

Simmer for 5 minutes, then whisk in 75g (2¾oz) of quick-cook polenta. Cook on a low heat for about 10 minutes, stirring every so often so that it doesn't stick to the bottom of the pan.

Add 60ml (2¼fl oz) of double cream and 75g (2¾oz) of freshly grated Parmesan and cook for a further 5 minutes.

BRAISED GOOSE IN RED WINE

MANY TIMES I RECOMMEND THAT THE WINE TO DRINK WITH THE DISH SHOULD BE THE ONE YOU USE IN ITS PREPARATION. However, having said that, I do not recommend using my first choice of wine in the sauce even though it is a triumph with the dish. The wine is a Barbaresco, from northern Italy, produced by Angelo Gaja. My preferred vineyard of his is Sori San Lorenzo (or Tildin). My preferred year? Well, in 1999 I drank the 1982 of this wine and it was one of the greatest liquid experiences of my life. It was at its peak (and drunk with freshly made pasta with pick-of-the-season white Piedmontese truffles). I would still pick a Barolo, Barbera or Barbaresco to go with this dish, of a vintage much younger, and the favoured producers are Gaja, and also Conterno (there are four of them in Alba, each different, each richly rewarding in its own way; they are Aldo, Giacomo, Paolo, and Claudio, though I must say my most sensual experiences have been with Aldo's wines), Ascheri, Pelissero, Spinetta, Michele Chiarlo, and Oddero. The prickle of roasted licorice in a Barbaresco or Barolo is wonderful – and the flavours of this dish do not overpower such wine but enhance it. These are also slightly craggy wines, and this is essential with a dish of such svelte richness and savour.

Does that sound paradoxical? On the contrary. A craggy wine can complement a svelte dish. Well, it does in this single instance, because it is not like meeting like. I often hear people say we're having a herby meal and so shouldn't we choose a herby wine? Or the dish is tangy so surely the wine must be? But the problem with reasoning like this is that like cancels out like, rather than complementing it. A wine and a food are, it is true, rarely capable of achieving so precise a fit, for neither is so exactly made as to be uniform every time. This surely adds, though, to the thrill of food and wine matching. The fits are endless, there are a myriad opportunities, and above it all rule the caprices of chance and personal taste. Will the wine be at its best? Will the dish turn out as expected?

And as for taste, who can legislate there? You may find my belief that Mark's goose goes with Barolo absurd. This is possible because each of us is an individual with a different number, and bias, of taste-buds and a wholly unique chemical disposition in our saliva. Both these factors are decisive in developing our likes and dislikes with flavours. I myself have an above average tolerance of acids. You may not. Taste is individual. Like you. Like the authors of this book. We will, then, never agree on everything. We disagree over lots of things.

WINE CHECKLIST

BAROLO (PIEDMONT – ITALY)

BARBARESCO (PIEDMONT – ITALY)

BARBERA (PIEDMONT – ITALY)

Morning Market Noodles

SERVES 4

IN THE MEKONG REGION OF SOUTHEAST ASIA, the early morning market stalls are literally steaming with women cooking up soups and noodles for shoppers and workers. Morning market noodles can consist of more or less what's available, but would be a base of fragrant broth to which you basically add what you want.

A nice thing to do for a dinner party is to have a bowl of broth over a table heater and a selection of greens, chicken, spring onions, and so on.

8 CHICKEN THIGHS, SKINNED | 4 CLOVES GARLIC, ROUGHLY CHOPPED | 1 ONION, QUARTERED | 10 BLACK PEPPERCORNS OR SICHUAN PEPPERCORNS | SMALL PIECE OF ROOT GINGER, PEELED AND ROUGHLY CHOPPED | 2 LIME LEAVES
TO SERVE
SALT AND/OR THAI FISH SAUCE, TO SEASON | 500G (1LB 2OZ) THIN, DRIED RICE NOODLES OR RICE VERMICELLI, SOAKED IN WARM WATER FOR 15 MINUTES, OR 1KG (2LB 4OZ) FRESH RICE NOODLES | 100G (3½OZ) BEAN SPROUTS | 250G (9OZ) CHINESE GREENS, SUCH AS PAK CHOI OR CHOI SUM, TRIMMED AND CUT INTO PIECES | BUNCH OF SPRING ONIONS, THINLY SLICED ON THE ANGLE | 2TBSP ROUGHLY CHOPPED CORIANDER LEAVES | 50G (1¾OZ) PEANUTS, LIGHTLY ROASTED AND CHOPPED
OPTIONAL CONDIMENTS
BLACK RICE VINEGAR | SOY SAUCE | ROASTED SESAME OIL | CHILLI SAUCE | FISH SAUCE | LIME WEDGES

1. To make the broth, put the chicken thighs in a large saucepan with the rest of the ingredients and cover with about 3 litres (5¼ pints) of water. Bring to the boil and simmer for 1 hour. Remove the chicken and leave to cool. Strain the stock through a fine-mesh sieve into a clean pan.

2. Simmer the stock until it's reduced by about one-third and has a good flavour. Season with some salt and/or a couple tablespoons or so of Thai fish sauce.

Remove the bones from the chicken and shred into chunky pieces. Add the chicken, noodles, bean sprouts, Chinese greens, spring onions, and coriander to the broth and simmer for 3–4 minutes with the lid on.

3. Serve in individual bowls or one large serving dish, scattered with peanuts, with the condiments of your choice.

NUTS

Nuts play a pretty important part in cooking for both desserts and savoury dishes. You can buy almost any nuts from any part of the world – shelled, roasted, and in their natural shells. As a natural product, they can help to emulsify sauces such as pesto or romesco sauce. They add texture to a crumble topping, or, toasted, they add a new dimension to desserts and salads. However, nuts are appearing less on menus these days as restaurateurs become more aware of the issue of nut allergies. I only came across it, as most of you probably did, some twelve or fourteen years ago. It never existed to my knowledge when I was at school, or if it did it was relatively unknown.

MORNING MARKET NOODLES

IT IS A MOOT POINT – CERTAINLY IT HAS BEEN THE SUBJECT OF HEATED SCIENTIFIC DEBATE SINCE THE LATE 1990s – whether or not minerals can find their way into a grape via the soil, but my view is that without question certain wines give the impression of minerality. As far as the nose and the palate are concerned, that's all we need for this dish: that citrusy, unripe-gooseberryish, minerally acidity of fine Kiwi Sauvignon Blanc to handle the spices and the fish sauce. Not just any old Kiwi Sauvignon either; we must be area-specific and look at Marlborough. For it was here, in the middle 1980s, that there emerged the first evidence of fine Sauvignon Blanc from the estate called Cloudy Bay. Sauvignon Blanc itself was never a fashionable grape in France until the mid-sixties, when it found favour among the artists and intellectuals who frequented La Coupole Brasserie in Paris. The wine was Sancerre. Personally, I had largely given up on Sancerre by the early 1980s, but when Cloudy Bay came along, and since then scores of other superb Kiwi Sauvignons, I discovered a more concentrated wine. For this dish, we need *le vrai* Sauvignon *de* Marlborough, and thus we must look for these names: Cloudy Bay, Jackson Estate, Hunter's, Grove Mill, Lawson's Dry Hills, plus at least a dozen others.

But there are other styles of wine which suit this dish if you want more fruit. Blue Ring Chardonnay from Western Australia is one such. This has a rich level of smoky melon and citrus fruit to handle those noodles superbly. The same goes for D'Arenberg Chardonnay from McLaren Vale. Both wines are sealed with screwcaps, and the youngest possible vintages should be paired with this dish.

WINE CHECKLIST

SAUVIGNON BLANC (MARLBOROUGH – NEW ZEALAND)

CHARDONNAY (MACLAREN VALE, SOUTH AUSTRALIA AND WESTERN AUSTRALIA)

WINE AND NUTS

Nuts and wine, as marriage prospects, play second fiddle to no one. In general, red wine (or a fortified wine such as port or madeira) works superbly with walnuts, roast chestnuts, cobnuts, brazils, pecans, even macadamias, and so on, and it is only when we come to peanuts that we find a nut which prefers to canoodle with a white wine. Try roast peanuts, without the noodles, with Gewurztraminer. You will be astonished at the union.

Chicken Kiev

SERVES 4

WHEN WAS THE LAST TIME YOU CUT THROUGH A CRUMBED CHICKEN BREAST AND A STREAM OF GARLIC BUTTER OOZED OUT? Chicken Kiev used to be commonplace on almost every menu with Steak Dianne and the likes, but now it's almost an endangered species, though you can find it in the freezer compartment in supermarkets. Properly done, it can be dreamy – there's always a reason why something was once so popular. But if this classic dish is prepared without due care you will end up with a dry old hollow bit of chicken and no gush of garlic butter. And that is probably why it went out of fashion. Time, then, to bring it back and show how good it can be.

4 CHICKEN BREASTS WITH THE WING BONE ON, SKINNED | 120G (4¼OZ) BUTTER, SOFTENED | 1TBSP FINELY CHOPPED NEW-SEASON GARLIC, OR 4 CLOVES ORDINARY GARLIC, CRUSHED | 2TBSP CHOPPED PARSLEY | SALT AND FRESHLY GROUND BLACK PEPPER | 3TBSP FLOUR | 1 LARGE EGG, BEATEN | 80–100G (2¾–3½OZ) FRESH WHITE BREADCRUMBS | VEGETABLE OR CORN OIL, FOR FRYING

1. Lay the chicken breasts with the small loose fillets facing upward. Remove the fillets with your fingers and put to one side. With a sharp filleting knife, cut two long incisions, away from the centre of the chicken breast, to form a pocket. Mix the butter, garlic, and parsley together and season. Put the mixture in the pocket, flatten the little fillet that was removed with the palm of your hand, and lay it over the butter. Fold the rest of the meat over the fillet and make sure it is sealed. Place in the refrigerator for 30–40 minutes.

2. Have three dishes ready: one with the flour, one with the beaten egg, and the third with the crumbs. Season the stuffed breasts and coat them in the flour, dusting off any excess, then put them through the egg, and finally the breadcrumbs.

   Preheat about 8cm (3¼ inches) of vegetable oil in a thick-bottomed saucepan or electric fryer to 160–180°C/325–350°F. Deep fry the chicken for 6–7 minutes until golden.

3. Serve with a vegetable such as creamed spinach, or a mixture of seasonal vegetables.

GARLIC

The mention of garlic can send people running. The idea of cooking with garlic is really for it to blend in with the rest of the flavours in the dish, rather than to overpower the main ingredient.

This is not always the case, though, and some kitchens will throw large amounts of garlic into a dish and mask the other flavours. Garlic must be treated with care and as far as possible be used fresh; don't use the bulbs that look as if they have been hanging around for months on end.

Garlic bulbs are not the only way of using garlic. In spring, wild garlic leaves, which grow along the side of the road and in woods, make a great addition to salads, soups, and sauces with a gentler flavour than the bulbs.

Garlic shoots can also be harvested without ruining the crop, and be chopped like spring onions and added to dishes. Similarly, garlic chives can be chopped and used in the same way. A good alternative is to bake whole heads of young garlic in foil and serve them with roast meats such as lamb and pork, or to scoop out the soft flesh and spread it on hot buttered toast.

CHICKEN KIEV

THIS IS A DISH WHICH SHOULDERS ITS WAY ONTO THE PALATE WITHOUT CEREMONY. This must be owing to the texture of the breadcrumbed component, that breast itself. But there is also significance in the fact that it has that highly aromatic, rich interior just waiting to burst out and define what it is we will discover on the end of our fork. Perhaps I am being excessively romantic, or even metaphysical, but I think this combination of rude exterior and hearty interior contributes to how we must select the wine. It, too, must be a surprise, and continue to fascinate us, take us by surprise, each time we smell and taste it. Otherwise, we have laboured vainly. For it is a dish which requires handling and getting into; and then chewing. Above all, then, we must find a wine with texture, having robustness without overly quirky rusticity or spiciness.

Merlot is an interesting grape to think of here, owing to its leatheriness: a textured, upholstered richness with a touch of luxury to it. French Merlots, from St-Emilion, say, may well have too many tannins for the job, but not those from Chile or New Zealand. André van Rensburg's "V", a blend of Médoc grapes (Cabernet Sauvignon, Merlot, and Cabernet Franc) from the Vergelegen Estate in South Africa, is an interesting choice, too, one of the greatest red wines not only of the Cape but also on the planet.

WINE CHECKLIST

MERLOT (CHILE AND NEW ZEALAND)

CABERNET SAUVIGNON/MERLOT/ CABERNET FRANC BLEND (SOUTH AFRICA)

WINE AND GARLIC

May I say something about garlic? It can be wholly discounted as an ingredient in a dish when it comes to deciding which wine to select. Even a plump fowl from Bresse in France, where the dishiest birds come from, has its wine chosen on the basis of the meat, not of the 150 cloves of garlic one famous recipe for it requires.

Only once has garlic dictated a wine choice, and that was when I was given, as a starter, a whole roasted head, the top sliced off, and a small spoon to scoop everything out. I chose a Provençal rosé to drink with it, and the other six diners thought it an inspired coupling.

Thai Green Chicken Curry

SERVES 4

THERE ARE SOME GOOD-QUALITY THAI GREEN CURRY PASTES ON THE MARKET. They give a good base to a Thai curry, especially when you haven't got an oriental grocer nearby. Try to buy an authentic one, which will probably be scribed in Thai. Look in your local supermarket's "special" range, and in particular for one by Charmaine Solomon, the authority on Asian cuisine. You can add various extra ingredients to a Thai curry such as pea aubergines – which are literally tiny, pea-sized aubergines – pumpkin, etc. It's also important not to miss out any of the spices as each adds its own character to the dish.

2TBSP **VEGETABLE OIL** | **SALT AND FRESHLY GROUND BLACK PEPPER** | 1KG (2LB 4OZ) **CHICKEN THIGH MEAT, SKINNED, BONED, AND HALVED IF LARGE** | 2 **ONIONS, ROUGHLY CHOPPED** | 2 **STICKS LEMON GRASS, TRIMMED AND FINELY CHOPPED** | 4 **CLOVES GARLIC, CRUSHED** | 30G (1OZ) **GALANGAL OR ROOT GINGER, PEELED AND FINELY CHOPPED** | 1TBSP **THAI GREEN CURRY PASTE** | 4 **LIME LEAVES** | 1.5 LITRES (2¾ PINTS) **CHICKEN STOCK** | 150ML (5FL OZ) **COCONUT MILK**
FOR THE FRESH GREEN PASTE
4 **LIME LEAVES** | **A FEW SPRIGS OF CORIANDER** | **A FEW SPRIGS OF THAI BASIL** | 1 **STICK LEMON GRASS, TRIMMED**

1. Heat the vegetable oil in a heavy-bottomed saucepan, season the chicken thighs, place them in the pan, and cook on a high heat for about 5–6 minutes. Add the onions, lemon grass, garlic, and galangal and continue cooking for another 5 minutes.

2. Add the curry paste, lime leaves, and chicken stock, bring to the boil, season, and simmer for 40 minutes. Meanwhile, blend the ingredients in a liquidizer for the fresh green paste with a tablespoon or so of water until smooth.

3. Add the coconut milk and fresh green paste to the curry, and simmer for about 10 minutes or until the sauce has thickened. Serve with jasmin or basmati rice.

CURRY

The UK's national dish deserves a bit of a mention here, as we eat more curry than roast beef or fish and chips. Not that they are really our national dishes either; but other countries just think they are.

The good old curry house has come a long way from those flock-wallpaper walls and a vindaloo after the pubs kick out – or has it? The curry movement is as popular as it's always been, and Indian chefs are now gaining recognition among other great cooks in London. Atul Kochhar, when he was at Tamarind, gained a star in the Michelin guide, and chefs such as Vineet Bhatia and Cyrus Todiwala among others are close behind.

The kormas and chicken tikka masalas are on the way out, and authentic cooking is back.

THAI GREEN CHICKEN CURRY

ONE INTERESTING CHOICE HERE IS VERDELHO FROM WESTERN AUSTRALIA (Bleasdale is excellent). Another is a Chenin Blanc from the Cape where the grapes have been a trifle late. And third, which surely heads the candidate list, is New Zealand Pinot Gris. What the coconut milk, basil, and galangal do to all these grapes is enhance their grapiness and very subtle spiciness; in return, the wine emphasizes – frames might be a shrewder way of terming it – the dish's ingredients, especially the lemon grass and chillies.

All in all, none of these happy, symbiotic occurrences can be achieved with any beer, which some people hold sacred with spicy oriental food. Beer simply wipes the palate clean. It adds nothing to the dish. It only takes away. By all means, enjoy beer as a wonderful, refreshing liquid – in some cases ponder its complexities and characterfulness but do not expect it to perform as only a wine can.

So, with Kiwi Pinot Gris taking precedence here, we look for a wine from producer Neil McCallum at Dry River. But can we find it? In a perfect world, yes. But it's not a perfect world and so we must find alternatives for this dish. Gewürztraminer, if it is young and frisky, is fine, and New World examples are certainly preferable to many from Alsace, unless you can get one from the co-op at Turckheim. This usually lacks the heaviness associated with this grape and provides a satiny-textured, genteel tanginess without an excess of spice. Perfect with this dish.

WINE CHECKLIST

PINOT GRIS (NEW ZEALAND)

VERDELHO (WESTERN AUSTRALIA)

CHENIN BLANC (SOUTH AFRICA)

GEWURZTRAMINER (ALSACE – FRANCE AND NEW WORLD)

WINE AND CURRY

Even among so-called civilized human beings (the last time was a conference of philosophers at London University), I am often greeted with scepticism when I propose that beer with curry is not a very good idea.

It does not enhance the food. It simply cleanses the palate. My favourite choices for the hot dishes of India, Pakistan, and Bangladesh are Aussie Shiraz, Californinan Zinfandel, and South African Pinotage. They do more than just cope. They get stuck in and add to the pleasure of eating the style of food.

Braised Rabbit with Mustard Sauce

SERVES 4

WILD RABBITS ARE UNDER-USED AT HOME, but with the number of bland battery chickens on the market they make a good, tasty alternative – although the thought of eating rabbit these days puts most people off, especially when they are kept as pets. Wild rabbits are generally sold whole in this country, whereas in France you can buy the various cuts. It seems a shame, though, to cook the saddles in a dish like this, as they take much less time than the legs to cook, and tend to be a bit dry. Remove the front and back legs, or get your butcher to do it, and keep the saddles for a salad. Once removed from the bone, the fillets take only a few minutes to cook and are really tender.

They make a great starter or main-course salad with some pan-fried black pudding, seasonal leaves, and a good mustard dressing. If wild rabbits are not available, there are some very tender – although not as well-flavoured – farmed rabbits on the market. They are also about twice the size of the wild ones, so one leg is almost enough for one person.

40G (1½OZ) FLOUR, PLUS EXTRA FOR DUSTING | 12 RABBIT LEGS (BACK ONLY), HALVED AT THE JOINT | SALT AND FRESHLY GROUND BLACK PEPPER | VEGETABLE OIL, FOR FRYING | 1 ONION, FINELY CHOPPED | 25G (1OZ) BUTTER | ½TBSP DIJON MUSTARD | ½TBSP GRAIN MUSTARD | 100ML (3½FL OZ) WHITE WINE | 750ML (1¼ PINTS) CHICKEN STOCK | 3TBSP DOUBLE CREAM | 1TBSP CHOPPED PARSLEY

1. Lightly flour the rabbit legs, and season with salt and pepper. Heat some vegetable oil in a frying pan and lightly brown the rabbit legs on both sides, then drain on some kitchen paper.

2. In a heavy-based saucepan, gently cook the onion in the butter until soft. Add the flour and stir well, then stir in the two mustards. Gradually pour in the wine, stirring well to avoid lumps, then pour in the chicken stock. Bring to the boil, add the rabbit legs, season and cover, and simmer gently for 1¼ hours, or until the rabbit is tender.

3. Remove the legs with a slotted spoon and set side. Add the cream to the cooking liquor and continue to simmer until the sauce has thickened. Put the legs back into the sauce, along with the chopped parsley, and bring back to the boil. Serve with mashed potatoes or mashed root vegetables.

MUSTARD
I always remember my grandfather Bill telling me how Colman's make their money from what is left on people's plates. Absolutely true, I reckon, and you just need to witness the plates coming back from the restaurant to confirm it. Like ketchup and other condiments, it's a personal thing to spoon mustard onto your plate – you either like it or you don't.

BRAISED RABBIT WITH MUSTARD SAUCE

WHAT A BITCH OF A DISH. Dijon and grain mustard! Well-known friends of wine. Ah well. Down the cellar we go. Hmm. I am tempted by old German Spätlesen, as the levels of sweetness and acidity of such wines (made from the Riesling grape) will combat those wicked ingredients, but who can acquire such wines in practice? My cellar has them in abundance, but then I adore such liquids. But this is the real world, and in the real world rabbit swings along with red wine, and so a red wine it will be. Interestingly, I suggest we chill the bottle. The Cabernet Franc grape will do us nicely, and those from the Loire's Chinon, Bourgueil, and Saumur-Champigny stand out. However, failing this, we must, turn to the organic vineyards of the Gallo Brothers in Sonoma where granddaughter Gina Gallo turns out terrific Cabernet Sauvignons from various individual vineyards as well as some wonderfully vivacious yet serious single-vineyard Zinfandels, like the one from Dry Creek in the photograph.

The latter wine, and not just Gina's, is terrific with a slightly gamey dish, like rabbit. I suppose the most famous Zinfandel from California is from Paul Draper's Ridge winery, and certainly Zins from there will accompany this dish extremely well. For many, indeed, it is Ridge Zinfandel which defines the breed. When I last experienced a Gina Gallo Zinfandel blind-tasted – that is to say, with the bottles disguised so the tasters knew not the origin – a most revealing incident occured. Having tasted both wines in bottles wrapped in brown paper, one bottle was found to be the unanimous preference of the wine snobs (excuse me! I mean wine writers) present. It was my choice also. I guessed it was Gina's wine. But one notable UK wine snob (sorry! I mean wine writer), believing his clear preference to be Paul's wine, because he could not imagine a wine with the word Gallo on it tasting so wonderful, tapped Gina on the head and said: "Well done, girl, but you'll never make a Zin as good as Paul Draper's". When the brown paper was torn off, the patronizing male chauvinist pig had to eat his words. He did so with style, I must say, with an enviable lack of shame.

WINE CHECKLIST

SPATLESE (ALL GERMAN REGIONS)

CABERNET FRANC (CHINON, BOURGUEIL, AND SAUMUR-CHAMPIGNY, LOIRE – FRANCE)

CABERNET SAUVIGNON (SONOMA, CALIFORNIA – THE USA)

ZINFANDEL (SONOMA, CALIFORNIA – THE USA)

WINE AND MUSTARD

Mustard, as is evident from my remarks above, is not always a friend to wine. This is not just because it is hot, sometimes very hot, but also because it contains vinegar (wine's deadliest enemy, because it is, of course, the other face of wine, what wine becomes when it reaches the stage of acetic acid). The cream and parsley in this dish, however, mitigate its effects deliciously, and render it wine's pal.

Classic Roast Duck

SERVES 4

IT'S IMPORTANT TO BUY A DECENT DUCK FOR THIS. Roasting a quality duck is fairly effortless as it takes little cooking and there is not too much fat to contend with. Serve this with some roast potatoes cooked in the pan with the duck.

2 GOOD-QUALITY DUCKS, EACH ABOUT 1.5–2KG (3LB 5OZ–4LB 8OZ) WITH THE NECKS, IF AVAILABLE | 1 ONION, QUARTERED | 1 LARGE CARROT, ROUGHLY CHOPPED | A FEW SPRIGS OF THYME | SALT AND FRESHLY GROUND BLACK PEPPER | ½TBSP FLOUR | HALF A GLASS OF WHITE WINE | 500ML (18FL OZ) BEEF OR CHICKEN STOCK | KNOB OF BUTTER

1. Preheat the oven to 220°C/425°F/Gas mark 7. Scatter the vegetables and thyme in a roasting tray. Season the ducks, sit them on the vegetables, and roast the birds for 1 hour, basting every so often.

2. For the gravy, tip away as much of the fat from the roasting tray as you can, then place the tray over a medium heat on the hob. Add the flour, then slowly stir in the wine and stock. Scrape up any sediment on the bottom of the pan and cook rapidly for a minute or so. Trransfer to a saucepan and simmer gently for 8–10 minutes, until it has reduced by about half and thickened.

3. Adjust the seasoning and sieve into a gravy boat or bowl. A little knob of butter stirred in at this point will give the gravy a nice sheen.

Remove the legs from the duck, take the breasts off the bone and slice them three or four times with a sharp knife, or chop the birds in half and serve them on the bone. Spoon the gravy over, and serve with apple sauce (below).

ACCOMPANIMENTS FOR ROASTS

Apple Sauce Melt a good knob of butter in a frying pan and sauté 650g (1lb 7oz) peeled, cored, and chopped apples with 15g (½oz) sugar for about 5 minutes, until the apples are nicely coloured and beginning to break down. Continue to stir the apples, then add 35g (1¼oz) sugar (you may not need it all, depending on how sweet the apples are) and cook for a few more minutes, until the apples are broken down but not completely puréed. Serve hot or cold with the meat.

Parsnip Chips Heat some vegetable or corn oil to 180°C/350°F in a deep-fat fryer or heavy-based saucepan. Using a sharp mandolin or vegetable peeler, slice 2 medium parsnips as thinly as possible lengthways. Rinse well, then pat them dry with a clean tea towel. Fry the slices in the hot oil a few at a time, stirring to ensure they don't stick together. The parsnips will take a while to colour and may appear soft while they are still in the fat, but once they have been drained they will dry out and crisp up. Drain on kitchen paper, sprinkle with salt, and leave them to dry somewhere warm, but not hot.

I always like to cook my stuffing inside the bird, as it collects all the cooking juices and tastes moist and delicious. Why people go to the trouble of making that packet stuff that tastes like reconstituted chippings from the floor of a bird cage I don't know.

Stuffing made at home can be effortless, and you just need to keep some fresh breadcrumbs in the freezer for your base. I like to add some sautéed onion and chopped chicken livers to my stuffing, but you can vary the mix as you wish. Thyme and parsley are my favourite herbs to use; they are not too overpowering and they complement the delicate texture of the bird.

CLASSIC ROAST DUCK

ONCE YOU SMEAR A FORKFUL OF DUCK OR CHICKEN, OR ANY SIMILAR GAMEY FOWL, DISHES WITH APPLE SAUCE, it is only a white wine which can survive the experience. A Tokay Pinot Gris from Alsace is superb with duck with a sweet sauce, and if the sauce really is sweet then a Gewurztraminer will also work well. If a red wine is what you prefer, then may I suggest one from the Fairview Estate in the Cape? Solitude Shiraz, certainly in the 2001 vintage which I tried, was a remarkable wine showing a grilled tomato aroma, big tannins of gripping yet civilized demeanour, a licorice undertone, and gorgeous chocolate fruit. The finish, so beautifully thick and textured, leaves the taster with the impression of having crunched mocha coffee beans (medium roast).

But there is another option, a brilliant, original, lip-smackin' option, with a dish like this, especially if the duck retains some of its succulent, savoury fat and the sauce is sweet apple. It is Aussie sparkling Shiraz. An excellent example is Wyndham Bin 555 Sparkling Shiraz, because not only is it sweetly vivacious with full-blown berries but also it has excellent biting tannins to give it oomph and serious food compatibility. Aussie sparkling Shiraz is one of the world's unsung heroes, as far as food matching is concerned, because it literally does fill a niche created by dishes like this which often are too sweet (owing to the sauce) for reds and too savoury (owing to the meat) for whites.

WINE CHECKLIST

TOKAY PINOT GRIS (ALSACE – FRANCE)

GEWURZTRAMINER (ALSACE – FRANCE)

SHIRAZ (SOUTH AFRICA)

SPARKLING SHIRAZ (AUSTRALIA)

Roast Partridge Stuffed with Cotechino

SERVES 4

COTECHINO IS A LARGE COARSE ITALIAN PORK SAUSAGE FLAVOURED WITH CLOVES AND CINNAMON. Available from delis, it's a speciality of northern Italy, traditionally served with lentils. It makes a good stuffing for game such as partridge, pigeon or wild duck. If you can't find it, you could use a traditional bread stuffing.

120G (4OZ) COTECHINO SAUSAGE | 250ML (9FL OZ) CHICKEN STOCK | 40G (1½OZ) FRESH WHITE BREADCRUMBS | 4 PARTRIDGES | SALT AND FRESHLY GROUND BLACK PEPPER | OLIVE OIL, FOR BASTING | 1 SMALL ONION, FINELY CHOPPED | 2 CLOVES GARLIC, CRUSHED | 1TSP THYME LEAVES | 1 SMALL CARROT, FINELY CHOPPED | GOOD KNOB OF BUTTER | 100ML (3½OZ) RED WINE | 40G (1½OZ) SPELT OR PEARL BARLEY, SOAKED FOR AN HOUR IN COLD WATER, COOKED FOR ABOUT 20 MINUTES IN SALTED WATER UNTIL TENDER, THEN DRAINED

1. Preheat the oven to 230°C/450°F/Gas mark 8. If the cotechino has any jelly on it, remove and add to the stock. Crumble up the sausage meat and mix it with the breadcrumbs. Remove any livers from the birds, chop them and mix with the stuffing. Fill the cavities of the partridges (not too tightly) with the stuffing and season the birds. Any remaining stuffing can be wrapped in foil and cooked with the partridges in the tray.

2. Brush the partridges with olive oil and roast for 15–20 minutes, giving them an occasional brush with more oil.

Meanwhile, gently cook the onion, garlic, thyme, and carrot in the butter for 3–4 minutes on a low heat until soft. Add the red wine and reduce by half, then pour in the stock and the cooked spelt or pearl barley and simmer until thickened.

3. To serve, halve the partridges, or leave whole, and serve with the sauce poured around them. Cavolo nero, Italian cabbage, is a good accompaniment.

OTHER GAME BIRDS

With most game, the flavour is down to the cooking – too long in the oven can totally destroy the flavours. Of all the seasonal foods, the game season is one of the most long awaited. The diversity of flavours among game birds is incredible, and probably why the game season is so exciting.

I love the classic accompaniments such as bread sauce and game chips, that are served with these birds, especially when it's in a posh place.

But, pheasant can go a bit dry, even when cooked perfectly. Although I did prepare a b'stilla with it once – which means long slow cooking with sweet and spicy flavours like almonds and cinnamon – and it was great, and a particularly good alternative to the more traditional pigeon.

ROAST PARTRIDGE STUFFED WITH COTECHINO

THIS IS A DISH TO BE EATEN THE NIGHT BEFORE THEY TAKE YOU OUT AND SHOOT YOU. It's a last-wish dish and requires a last-wish wine. Let me offer some ideas.

The first is Auguste Clape's Cornas Renaissance, of a vintage of some four to eight years' antiquity. This is a 100 per cent Syrah from a particular spot in the northern Rhône where the surrounding hillside vines of Cornas enjoy a sheltered situation which not only mitigates the worst of the mistral – the often devastating wind of the region (and of Provence) – but also keeps the temperatures higher during the day. Tannins build up, as they also do during the nights (which can be cool in early season), and so with a grower like Clape a wine of pedigree, character, and heft is created which is berried up to its neck in fruit.

We now turn to other Syrahs, or more correctly Shirazes, and for this we cross the planet, and alight in McLaren Vale, and look for producers D'Arenberg, Leasingham, Wirra Wirra, and Coriole. The Lloyd Reserve Shiraz from Coriole can be utterly magnificent, and with this dish, perfect.

The best last-wish wine, however, could be a Bass Phillip Pinot Noir from Gippsland in Victoria, one three to five years old. A rare wine? To be sure. But it is made by the King of Australasian Pinot. His very name, Phillip Jones, sends a frisson of excitement down the tongues of the cognoscenti, and a languid shiver of fear to engulf the spines of other competitive Pinot producers. His sassiest wines, bearing the label Bass Phillip, can cost AUS$300 in Aussie bottle shops and restaurants. AUS$380 was the price of a bottle of his finest in a Melbourne restaurant in 2002, and it was the most concentrated, aromatic, beautifully textured Pinot I had tasted since Jean Gros Richebourg of 1972. Phillip Jones has a thrillingly saggy face (his bags have eyes rather than vice versa) and a voice like gravel being scraped along the side of an iron pot. He is more committed to Pinot Noir than any other human being I have ever met, including many (perhaps all) of the soi-disant champions of this grape, the Burgundians.

WINE CHECKLIST

SYRAH (NORTHERN RHONE – FRANCE)

SHIRAZ (MCLAREN VALE – SOUTH AUSTRALIA)

PINOT NOIR (GIPPSLAND, VICTORIA – AUSTRALIA)

5
Desserts

AROUND THE WORLD, DESSERTS AND DESSERT CULTURE VARY MASSIVELY, from being almost non-existent in some Asian countries to consisting of over-sweet concoctions elsewhere. Personally, I have become bored with modern desserts, and if I had the choice I would go for an old-fashioned, British nursery pudding any day. But, I must admit, I much prefer savoury to sweet things unless I have a chocolate craving, and that generally isn't at the end of a meal. Sugar tends to work its way into most desserts and can take over all other flavours, except, of course, the delicious burned sugar on a crème brûlée.

Dessert-making is a bit of an art, a specialist subject that many professional cooks never explore – that is, some chefs stick to the savoury stuff, and pastry chefs tend just to do pastry. It needs accurate measures and spot-on temperatures, whereas sauce-

> Dessert-making is a bit of an art. It needs accurate measures and spot-on temperatures.

making and cooking meat and fish needs a certain feel and good taste-buds. But you can be a bit more adventurous with desserts, unlike starters and main courses. Mixing and matching flavours and textures can be exciting – you will find that meat and fish don't quite work in the same way. There are certain combinations that just don't work together, and others that marry up perfectly. With desserts, the possibilities are endless.

MY THEORY ABOUT PUDDINGS AND WINE IS BASED ON THE NOTION THAT THIS MARRIAGE COMES AT THE WORST POSSIBLE TIME – after several courses and wines have already been enjoyed. It is rather like going on honeymoon when the partners have already enjoyed ten wonderful years together. How can anyone enjoy a bread and butter pudding with a magnificent Sauternes or a fantastic Californian or Aussie stickie after a meal begun with, say, spicy Thai fish soup with New Zealand Pinot Gris, followed by steak pie with South African Cabernet Sauvignon, a succulent Aussie Shiraz with the cheese, and then that pud?

You get my point. So, one solution is to build the meal backward. One day I was given a wonderful apple tart made by a friend, with superbly thin pastry, and Calvados in the burned butter in the apples. I resolved to serve a twenty-nine-year-old German Riesling Beerenauslese with it. Before this, I offered rough country pâté with chilled Teroldego Rotaliano from Trentino in north Italy – a modest but characterful red wine – and a huge green salad. A long pause, and then arrived that tart. With noses in glasses my guests simply swooned around the table, and the dessert disappeared as did three bottles of the wine.

If the pudding is an afterthought, do not go beyond simple sweet wines like Moscatel de Valencia. If the pudding is sensational, lead up to it shrewdly.

The moral of this story? If the pudding is an afterthought, do not go beyond simple sweet wines like Moscatel de Valencia. If the pudding is sensational, as Mark's are, then lead up to it shrewdly, so it is a genuine course by itself. Then the wine can be equally sensational.

Sussex Pond Pudding

SERVES 4–6

I LOVE THIS PUDDING BECAUSE IT'S MESSY BUT FULL OF FLAVOUR. You can't believe it is going to work, with a whole fruit in the middle of the pudding. But the lemon serves two purposes: it holds up the pudding at the same time as the flavour filters into the buttery sauce and into the pastry as it cooks. When you turn it out, the dish becomes a pond of delicious sweet lemony syrup. You will need a 1 litre (1¾ pint) pudding basin, string and foil.

250G (9OZ) SELF-RAISING FLOUR | 125G (4½OZ) SHREDDED BEEF SUET OR VEGETABLE SUET | 150ML (5FL OZ) MILK | 300G (10½OZ) UNSALTED BUTTER, SOFTENED, PLUS EXTRA FOR GREASING | 200G (7OZ) SOFT LIGHT BROWN SUGAR | 1 LARGE UNWAXED LEMON

1. Combine the flour and suet together in a bowl. Mix into a dough with the milk. The dough should be soft but sufficiently firm to roll out into a circle large enough to line the pudding basin. Cut a quarter out of the circle, so that you can make a cone shape with the dough to fit more easily in the pudding basin, leaving you left-over dough for the lid. Put this slice of dough aside. Butter the pudding basin well and drop the pastry into it, flattening it at the bottom, and joining up the edges where the slice was taken out.

2. Mix the butter and sugar together and put into the lined basin. Prick the lemon all over as much as you can, with a roasting fork or skewer, so that the juices can escape, and push it into the butter mixture. Roll the remaining pastry out into a circle to fit the top of the basin. Lay it over the filling, and press the edges of the dough together to seal. Take a piece of foil big enough to fit over the basin with at least an extra 5cm (2 inches) overlapping. Make a pleat down the middle of the foil, place it over the top of the basin, and tie in place with string round the top edge, or like a parcel with a string handle, so it can be lifted into and out of a saucepan.

3. Bring a large pan half-filled with water to the boil and lower in the pudding. Cover and leave to simmer for 4 hours. Don't let the water stop boiling. If the level drops, lift the basin out and top up with more boiling water.

To serve, lift out, remove the foil and loosen the sides with a small sharp knife. (The pudding can be kept hot for another hour or so until it's needed.) Put a deep dish over the basin and quickly turn the whole thing upside down.

CITRUS FRUIT

The lemon has many uses in the kitchen, from its citrus qualities and flavourings to its high content of vitamin C, which is used to stop foods discolouring before or during cooking. The rind, or zest, as it's more commonly known, has a different flavour from the juice and can be added to sauces, dressings, cakes, pastries, and custards without affecting the consistency, giving them an intense citrus flavour without the sourness of the juice.

The lime has similar qualities and can be used in exactly the same way as lemon. It's especially used for giving dishes an extra sour note.

DOMAINE
DE LA
TAILLE AUX LOUPS
2003
ONTLOUIS SUR LOIRE
PPELLATION MONTLOUIS SUR LOIRE CONTRÔLÉE
en bouteille à la propriété
JACKY BLOT

SUSSEX POND PUDDING

THIS PUD HAS SEVERAL STICKING QUALITIES. It adheres to the spoon. It hangs about, deliciously, on the palate. It lingers in the throat. The wine to stay this course, therefore, cannot be light or lightly chosen. However, if this wine is too clotted, an ancient Sauternes, say, we duplicate some of the aspects of the dish itself. Contrast is required. This is best found in the acidity of the accompanying wine, not its level of sweet fruitiness. Youth is a factor, then, as is a variety of grapes: Riesling, Chenin Blanc, Pinot Gris.

My first choice for this dish is a sweet Loire white (Chenin Blanc) from Vouvray, Coteaux du Layon, Quarts-de-Chaume, Bonnezeaux, or Montlouis (Jacky Blot is the name to look for here among several other outstanding producers). You could also go for a Coteaux de Saumur, another sweet Chenin Blanc-based white, but this wine is much harder to find (unless you're resident in the Loire). These wines are, to my mind and pocket, not just a discrete acreage of French white wine greatness, but one of the vinous world's loveliest, and, in some respects, least appreciated, treasures. Often graced with noble rot, where the berries are left on the vine to dehydrate, and attract a fungus which concentrates the sugars as well as bequeathing a richness of its own which gives the resulting wine a delicious caramel or butterscotch character, such wines offer magnificently complex acidity harnessed to fruit which recalls peaches, raspberries, apples, pears, and honey, and there is a butterscotch undertone to the whole thrilling ensemble.

Bonnezeaux can be brilliant, but even better can be Quarts-de-Chaume, a mere 48 hectares or so of vines split between myriad owners, for such wines develop with age the level of intensity and acid/honey balance of the more famous Sauternes or Trockenbeerenauslesen. But in the end I turn to that Montlouis *moelleux*, nowhere near as tart or sweet as a Trockenbeerenauslese, but with the oiliness to survive, just, that suet pud. And desserts with citrus fruit in their make-up go well with such wines.

WINE CHECKLIST

BONNEZEAUX (LOIRE – FRANCE)

QUARTS-DE-CHAUME (LOIRE – FRANCE)

MONTLOUIS MOELLEUX (LOIRE – FRANCE)

Riesling Jelly with Summer Fruit

SERVES 4

I'VE BECOME A BIT OF A JELLY NUT. Jellies are great and so adaptable to the seasons. In the summer, you can flavour the jelly with anything from elderflowers to Champagne, and when the winter is close, apple juice and blackberries are a good way to use up the tail-end of the berries. I once made an absinthe jelly for a dinner party with some friends and used about 50 degrees of alcohol to sugar syrup – that really got the party going, as you can well imagine.

JUICE OF HALF A LEMON | 150G (5½OZ) CASTER SUGAR | 5 SHEETS LEAF GELATINE | 250ML (9FL OZ) RIESLING | 120G (4¼OZ) SUMMER FRUIT SUCH AS RASPBERRIES, SLICED STRAWBERRIES, BLUEBERRIES, REDCURRANTS, BLACKBERRIES

1. Bring 300ml (10fl oz) of water and the lemon juice to the boil. Add the sugar and stir until dissolved, then remove from heat. Soak the gelatine leaves in a shallow bowl of cold water for a minute or so until soft. Squeeze out the water and add the gelatine to the syrup along with the Riesling. Stir until dissolved.

2. Put the jelly somewhere cool, but do not let it set. Fill individual jelly moulds, or one large one, with half the berries, then pour in half of the cooled jelly. Put in the refrigerator for an hour or so to set, then top up with the rest of the berries and unset jelly. This allows the berries to stay suspended and not float to the top. Return to the refrigerator. To serve, turn out, and offer thick Jersey cream to go with it.

SUMMER FRUIT

Summer fruit are well worth waiting for. Unfortunately, though, they are now available imported for most of the year, and it won't be long before we have forgotten when the berry season really starts. We are getting used to grabbing them at any time of the year off the supermarket shelves. They generally tend not to have the flavour of the seasonal fruit, although some of them are available to us in the season of their country of origin and will have some flavour. For me, berries are best served simply without any other intruding flavours, except some thick pouring or clotted cream.

RIESLING JELLY WITH SUMMER FRUIT

THIS REALLY IS A CHUNK OF HEDONISM ON A PLATE. In the glass set beside it, mere utilitarian notions must be discarded. Any old dessert wine will not do. Luxury is required, cost irrelevant; a marriage of like substances is essential, and so we must tread emphatically yet delicately and bring up from the cellar a bottle of Torcolato, the Italian sweetie. This white can hardly pass itself off as merely white, for it is a deep gold in hue, made from Tocai, Vespaiolo, and Garganega grapes in the Veneto. It is made from half-dried berries (*passito*), and, with age (not anywhere near as long as with other sweet wines), it offers some delicious honey and tropical fruitiness with an underlying hint, in some vintages, of candied cherries.

Botrytis, the so-called noble rot, can also be present in the grapes, so they are already dehydrated before being picked and left to dry further. The only producer of this wine whose liquids I am familiar with over several years of tasting is Faustino Maculan. Now, I appreciate this wine doesn't grow on trees and won't be found in every street-corner bottle shop, and so, in its absence, I can certainly recommend Brown Brothers Orange Muscat and Flora from the state of Victoria, Australia. This sweetie, when young, is excellent with this dessert.

Indeed, some young, exuberant savants of the vine aver that this Victorian wine is superior to many fine sweet Bordeaux. I am inclined to agree, except I must add that I judge the wine as a companion to this dish. And as such it is superior, because it has a devil-may-care, honeyed richness which summer fruits love so well.

WINE CHECKLIST

PASSITO WHITE (VENETO – NORTHEAST ITALY)

ORANGE MUSCAT AND FLORA (VICTORIA – AUSTRALIA)

Rhubarb Tart with Elderflower Cream

SERVES 4

THIS IS BASED ON THE CLASSIC TARTE FINE AUX POMMES, and the rhubarb works just as well as apples. I served it to some friends at a dinner party – they weren't rhubarb lovers at all, but they still managed to leave clean plates. Try to select rhubarb stems that are bright red and of an even thickness, as the end result will look better. I wouldn't bother making your own puff pastry for this tart, as the pastry is rolled so thin you won't notice.

APPROX 150–180G (5½–6½OZ) PUFF PASTRY, ROLLED TO ⅓CM (⅛ INCH) THICK |
500G (1LB 2OZ) MEDIUM-SIZED DEEP RED RHUBARB | **1TBSP CASTER SUGAR**
FOR THE SYRUP
TRIMMINGS FROM THE RHUBARB | **2TBSP CASTER SUGAR**
FOR THE CREAM
100ML (3½FL OZ) DOUBLE CREAM | **1TBSP CASTER SUGAR** | **1TBSP ELDERFLOWER CORDIAL**

1. Cut four 12x8cm (4½x3¼-inch) rectangles from the pastry and put them onto a nonstick baking tray. Cut the rhubarb into 11cm (4¼-inch) lengths and lay them on top of the pastry as close to each other as possible, leaving 5mm (¼ inch) of pastry all the way round. Preheat the oven to 220°C/425°F/Gas mark 7. Sprinkle the sugar over the rhubarb and bake for 15–20 minutes until the pastry is crisp. If the rhubarb starts to colour too much, turn the oven down.

2. Meanwhile, put the rhubarb trimmings in a pan along with the sugar and simmer together for 8–10 minutes, stirring every so often. Strain the liquid through a fine meshed sieve, pushing all the liquid through with the back of a spoon into a clean pan (do not discard the bits of rhubarb). Boil this liquid until it has reduced by about half and has begun to thicken. Remove from the heat and leave to cool.

3. Whisk the cream, sugar, and elderflower cordial together until stiff peaks form, then carefully fold in about a tablespoon of the rhubarb bits from the strained sauce. The rest can be discarded. Serve the tart with a spoonful of the cream mixture and some of the syrup.

PASTRY

Pastry is a versatile thing for both sweet and savoury dishes. If you are not confident with pastry-making you can actually buy most types of pastry ready-made these days, and even ready-rolled. So, knocking up a tart or pie doesn't have to be such a tedious task after all.

Pastry-making is a bit of a touch-and-feel affair; you can give two people the same pastry recipe and the results will be completely different. I always remember my grandmother making pastry with lard and butter for a less rich but more crumbly finish to her pastry.

Pastry recipes are never-ending and often confusing. The simplest recipes with the least number of ingredients normally work the best, as there is less to go wrong. There is a bit of a science to pastry, and pastry recipes are less easy to fix than, say, a sauce recipe or a soup.

RHUBARB TART WITH ELDERFLOWER CREAM

IT IS MOST ADVANTAGEOUS TO PARTNER THIS DISH WITH A SWEET, LATE-HARVEST RIESLING from the Rhine, Nahe or Mosel. Or, in the case of D'Arenberg Noble Riesling, from McLaren Vale in South Australia. This is a tricky little pud, delicious but more dainty than you might suspect, and a degree of delicacy is necessary in the wine. That is to say, if it is too full-on sweet and rich, it will smother this dessert like a sauce. Something is required which will enhance the pudding and, between mouthfuls, enhance the experience of its lingering presence. Acidity, not sugar, is what is required, and in Riesling we get it (unless the wine is heavily honeyed, like an old Trockenbeerenauslese).

Another idea is *vin santo*, the Tuscan dessert wine. The greatest one I have tasted was from Castello Brolio, of the 1947 vintage. It is doubtful if you will find one of such antiquity outside a visit to Brolio itself or an auction, but younger vintages are more widely available, and there are several producers. The 1947 was sensational, and I am afraid I did a greedily vulgar thing after having tasted two glasses at a dinner at Brolio. I waited for everyone else in the room to vacate their seats to go and see a fireworks display, and I went round the room and snaffled up all the half-empty glasses and filled a large burgundy glass two-thirds full. I can't abide waste of a beautiful object, and this *vin santo* was the finest and most fluent I have ever tasted. *Vin santo* is made from partially dried grapes, and it has, when young, an acidic edge (perfect with rhubarb of course), but after fifty-six years it mellows (don't we all?), and in this specimen the honeyed richness had gone like burned toffee with molasses and cream. Quite why so many people left their glasses barely touched I shall never understand.

Still, I enjoyed my fill of it, and it went with the fireworks splendidly. This latter phenomenon was the most excitingly entertaining I have witnessed, helped by the fact that the castle was so high and the pyrotechnicians were so low that one could see all the display without lifting one's head – except to drain the *vin santo*. All other types of sweet pastry work equally well with these wines.

WINE CHECKLIST

LATE-HARVEST RIESLING (RHINE, NAHE, AND MOSEL – GERMANY)

NOBLE RIESLING (MCLAREN VALE – SOUTH AUSTRALIA)

VIN SANTO (TUSCANY – ITALY)

Iced Berries with Hot White Chocolate Sauce

SERVES 4

THIS IS ONE OF THOSE PERFECT MARRIAGES OF INGREDIENTS, and one of the easiest desserts to prepare and serve. The idea came from a customer just back from a skiing trip. I can't think why more chefs haven't copied it. Maybe it's because it's not stretching enough for most pastry chefs. But when it comes to producing a beautiful dessert at home, this is the one. And what could be simpler: excess berries you may have gathered from the garden in the summer, just waiting for the moment to be coated in white chocolate sauce.

You can serve this in summer or winter, and, if you haven't gathered your own, most supermarkets stock a selection of berries or individual ones, but do avoid serving large berries such as strawberries, unless they are sliced, or there may be a trip to the dentist in store.

300G (10½OZ) BEST-QUALITY WHITE CHOCOLATE, BUTTONS OR BARS, CHOPPED INTO PIECES |
300ML (10FL OZ) DOUBLE CREAM | 500G (1LB 2OZ) FROZEN MIXED SMALL BERRIES

1. Put the chocolate and cream into a bowl over a pan of simmering water for about 20–30 minutes, stirring every so often. This can be done while you are eating your starters or mains. When the sauce is hot, just cover it with clingfilm and turn the heat off.

2. Five minutes before serving, put the berries onto dessert plates and leave at room temperature to lose a little of their chill.

Transfer the chocolate sauce into a serving jug. Place the berries in front of your guests and pour the hot chocolate sauce generously over the berries.

TART DARK BERRIES

Although I've said that most berries need very little doing to them, there are a few exceptions that do require a little more attention. Currants – red, black, and white – blackberries, and gooseberries are rarely that sweet, unless you have picked them yourself in peak condition, so invariably they need to be cooked with sugar or mixed with other fruit, such as a blackberry and apple pie, for example. Jams and jellies are also a good way to use up surplus harvest, and they can be delicious used as an accompaniment to cheeses or game and lamb dishes. Redcurrants can also be dropped into a sauce at the last minute to go with game or duck, and even stirred into a dressing and tossed with some salad leaves for a fruity summer salad with lamb or duck fillets. So don't rule out the tartness of those tricky berries – they have many uses.

ICED BERRIES WITH HOT WHITE CHOCOLATE SAUCE

THIS MOULD-BREAKING DESSERT REQUIRES A MOULD-BREAKING WINE. Further, it will benefit from a wine it was surely created to partner. Chocolate, I am half-persuaded to admit, is a hobby of mine. I consume organic Green & Black's on a daily basis. I even attend chocolate tastings. Here is an extract from my chocolate-tasting notebook:"Spend the early part of the evening eating chocolates in the so-called Chinese Room at the Mirabelle restaurant in Mayfair. All part of a rich day's work. The chocolate is called El Rey (presumptuous, but that's the world of confectionery for you) and it comes from Venezuela. It is apparently the only chocolate in the world to be made from 100% Carenero cacao beans which, also apparently, connoisseurs reckon are the bee's knees. I spend a hedonistic few hours nibbling all manner of chocolate fantasies, made by leading chocolatiers in the UK, the USA, and Japan. The ones I dig the most and reckon the grooviest are made by L.A. Burdick who mixes his chocolates in the little New Hampshire town of Walpole."

Now, you will ask what, if anything, do I take from all this indulgence from the wine point of view? Well, with those El Rey chocolates I tasted twenty-year-old tawny port, madeira, Aussie honeyed white wine and red Shiraz, Chilean Merlot, sherry, and Glenmorangie malt whisky. I found that the best wines in the world to go with chocolate come from Catalan France: Banyuls and Maury – sweet reds from Roussillon, look for Domaine de Mas Blanc Banyuls and Banyuls l'Etoile cooperative.

From Hungary, Tokaj Aszu, if it is 5 Puttonyos and ten years old (or preferably more), can also be companionable (*see also* page 165). The tawny port and madeira can handle this dessert only if they are very sweet and very old.

WINE CHECKLIST

BANYULS (ROUSSILLON – FRANCE)

MAURY (ROUSSILLON – FRANCE)

TOKAJ ASZU 5 PUTTONYOS (HUNGARY)

TAWNY PORT, 20 OR 30-YEAR-OLD (PORTUGAL)

WINE AND DARK BERRIES
The addition of berries to any ice-cream or chocolate recipe increases the level of acidity in the dish and it depends on the level of this acidity as to whether one wine rather than another should be preferred. Dark berries are more concentrated and in general I would go for a sweet wine that is mature rather than young. This is because older dessert wines are deeper and counteract the richer acidity in the dish.

Chocolate Fondue with Churros

SERVES 4–6

AS A KID I REMEMBER A MOBILE VAN COMING DOWN TO THE SEAFRONT AT WEST BAY SELLING SOME WEIRD, HORSESHOE-SHAPED DOUGHNUTS. It was a bit way out for deepest Dorset, but I got a bit hooked on them as they seemed an unusual treat at the time. They were simply dredged with granulated sugar and served in a paper bag. I always thought, before I became a food nut, that they were made of some sort of potato concoction, and later discovered they were just simply a form of choux pastry, deep fried. There was no melted chocolate to dip them into, even though fondue parties were the rage then.

100G (3½OZ) PLAIN FLOUR | 2TBSP OLIVE OIL | 1TSP CASTER SUGAR | 1TSP SALT | 2 EGGS, BEATEN | OIL, FOR DEEP FRYING | GRANULATED SUGAR, FOR COATING
FOR THE FONDUE
200G (7OZ) GOOD-QUALITY DARK CHOCOLATE | 150ML (5FL OZ) DOUBLE CREAM

1. Sift the flour onto a sheet of foil – it will make it easier to pour when the time comes. Put 150ml (5fl oz) of water, the oil, sugar, and salt into a saucepan and bring to the boil. Remove from the heat. Holding the corners of the foil, pour in the flour and beat in with a wooden spoon to form a smooth paste. Return to a low heat and stir for 2–3 minutes until the mixture leaves the sides of the pan in a firm ball of paste. Remove from the heat and leave to cool for a couple of minutes.

2. In a food mixer with a paddle, or by hand, gradually beat in the eggs a little at a time until the mixture is smooth. Remove the mixture with a spatula into a piping bag fitted with a 1cm (½-inch) star nozzle.

Meanwhile, heat 8cm (3¼ inches) of vegetable oil to 160ºC/320°F in a deep-fat fryer or heavy-bottomed deep pan. Carefully pipe the dough into the oil in 6cm (2½-inch) lengths, using a small knife to cut the mixture. Cook until golden and crisp.

3. Remove onto some kitchen paper with a slotted spoon, dredge with granulated sugar, and prepare to eat immediately. You can cook these beforehand if you are making a lot, and just dip them back into hot fat before you serve them.

Meanwhile, put the chocolate and double cream in a double boiler or a bowl over a pan of hot water until it has melted. Serve the chocolate in a fondue pot, or in a heatproof dish over a table warmer, with the hot churros to dunk.

CHOCOLATE

Chocolate has become a great social subject, and we are all becoming chocolate snobs. That's a good thing though, because we have finally come round to the fact that a bar of chocolate does not have to be sweet and full of unnecessary flavourings to tempt our conservative palates anymore. Chocolate purists will now only buy chocolate that boldly displays at least seventy per cent cocoa solids on the packet, and we find ourselves sifting through the shelves to find topnotch stuff for treats for the kids – in small quantities, of course, because the real thing doesn't come cheap. Even hot chocolate has taken a turn for the better, and my girls, Ellie and Lydia, are enjoying the goo of freshly melted chocolate in their breakfast-time drink.

CHOCOLATE FONDUE WITH CHURROS

A SWEET OLOROSO SHERRY IS MARVELLOUS HERE. Just run the word around your tongue for a moment. Oloroso. Is it not a delicious sound? Does it not suggest opulence and congeniality merely as it rolls off the tongue? *Oll-low-row-so*. The word has two further virtuous dimensions. One is its appearance on the page. Just look at it. Isn't oloroso a sketch of a railway locomotive? Consider that protuberant lower-case "l"; the profusion of "o"s; the linking curvatures of the "r" and the "s". And then consider, above all, that the word merely means fragrant in Spanish, and you have it: the perfect wine to go with this dish. Yes, I know oloroso is a sherry, and such a thing is deeply unfashionable, but really, it is a wonderful wine, and in its sweetened versions, which we need for churros, perfect.

There are several producers' offerings to choose from, but twist my arm and I will go for Gonzalez-Byass Matusalem. It is one of the world's greatest sherries. The texture and the colour of engine oil, it has a butterscotch and crème brûlée sweetness, and a complex, smoky, honeyed edge. Earthlings often speculate what the drink of the gods might have been like, what Nectar (so-called) must have tasted like, and Matusalem is my best guess. I say this because it surely confers immortality on all who drink it, just as the food of the gods, Ambrosia, was said to do.

WINE CHECKLIST

**SWEET OLOROSO SHERRY
(SOUTHWEST – SPAIN)**

WINE AND CHOCOLATE

Is there any difference, when it comes to choosing a wine, whether the chocolate is dark, white or milk? I can report on my years of research with bars of chocolate that I have discovered that the best match for pure-dark chocolate is an old, rich sherry, like Gonzalez-Byass's Noe; with milk chocolate I like a ten- or twenty-year-old tawny port; and with white chocolate I tend to go for marsala – the sweet wine from Sicily.

Tarte à la Crème

SERVES 4

THIS IS PROBABLY THE FRENCH EQUIVALENT OF A SIMPLE CUSTARD TART. It hits the spot for a simple but indulgent dessert, or an afternoon tea pastry. I've tried it with normal cream, but the flavour just doesn't get close to the versions I've sampled in France – probably because the French don't have the style of fresh double cream we have in the UK, and much of their cream is long-life, the type that's not refrigerated. You can buy it here – you will need to look for long-life cream.

200G (7OZ) PUFF PASTRY | 700ML (1¼ PINTS) UHT DOUBLE CREAM | 70G (2¼OZ) CASTER SUGAR | 1 VANILLA POD, SPLIT AND SEEDS SCRAPED OUT

1. I wouldn't recommend making one large tart as it could be messy to cut into slices and serve, so you'll need enough individual tart tins. Roll the pastry to ½cm (⅛-inch) thick, and prick it all over with a fork. Line four 10x2cm (4x¾-inch)-deep tart cases with the pastry, and line them with greaseproof paper or foil, then with baking beans to stop them rising. Leave to rest for at least an hour in the fridge. Preheat the oven to 180°C/350°F/Gas mark 4.

2. Put the cream into a saucepan with the sugar, vanilla pod, and seeds. Bring to the boil and simmer, stirring with a whisk every so often until it has reduced by half and thickened.

   Bake the tarts for 15 minutes, then remove the baking beans and cook for a further 5 minutes. Remove from the oven and leave to rest for 5 minutes before removing them from the tins.

3. Discard the vanilla, scraping away any seeds. Fill the tarts with the mixture and leave to set in the fridge. Serve with strawberries or raspberries or a selection of berries. It doesn't need any more cream with it!

CREAM AND VANILLA

What a harmonious marriage. They were just made for each other. In a custard, an ice-cream, or a milkshake they just work. The vanilla pod is up there in the luxury spice bracket. You don't get many pods for your money, so treat them with care and respect. Buy just what you need, and don't leave them lying around in your larder for too long. The pods should be soft and subtle when you buy them, and they are often sold in handy little test-tube containers.

Once you have scraped the seeds out for a custard and infused the pods in the cream or milk, just hold on; they are not ready for the bin yet. Wash them off, dry them out, and just stick them into a Kilner jar with some caster sugar to infuse for the next time you make a custard or even a vanilla ice-cream. Get your money's worth! It's probably the only spice you can recycle and get away with in this fashion. Imagine trying to wash saffron strands!

TARTE A LA CREME

MOSCATEL DE VALENCIA, WITH ITS SCREWTOP, IS A NATURAL PARTNER FOR THIS DISH. Of course, pedants can argue, with some justification, that this wine is not a wine at all, and no strict court of law can deny them their case. This is on the grounds that wine must be over 5 degrees of alcohol, and Moscatel de Valencia only achieves this by virtue of blending grape brandy with the barely fermented must of Muscat grapes (well under 5 degrees of alcohol before the spirit is added to bring the alcohol level of the bottled product up to 15 degrees). Look for "Moscatel" rather than a producer.

I am not a pedant. I seek only perfection of the vinous partner in the food-wine marriage, and here we have it: a wine providing immediate lashings of slightly herby honey with an undertone of marmalade. It has the further virtue of being cheap, hardly a fraction of the price of the great Barsacs and Sauternes or Monbazillacs, which you could, if you concurred with the pedants' argument, drink with this dessert. Château d'Yquem is the greatest Sauternes, at least in reputation (not always in aroma and taste), and it is the most expensive, because each of the estate's vines produces just one glass of the unctuous liquid. Other names to look for in the Sauternes and Barsacs are Lafaurie-Peyraguey (my favourite), Climens, Coutet, and Doisy-Daëne (also a personal favourite).

As for Monbazillac – an underrated sweet wine, some examples of which easily challenge the greatest Bordeaux – I am enormously fond of Domaine de l'Ancienne Cure, Châteaux de la Haute-Brie et du Caillou (not easily available), Château le Fagé (scrumptious!), and Château le Mayne. There are many others. Let me just say that the great Sauternes and Barsacs, though on their day among the most complete and complex of sweeties, have not, in my experience, always been able to live with the rich desserts that often the more waxily textured of the richest Monbazillacs can combat with ease.

Which leaves us the ravishing sweet wine in the photograph: Barbadillo Sticky Pudding Wine from the sherry region in Spain. It is a triumph of treacly richness and nutty complexity – and sublime with Mark's dessert.

WINE CHECKLIST

MOSCATEL DE VALENCIA (SPAIN)

BARSAC (BORDEAUX – FRANCE)

SAUTERNES (BORDEAUX – FRANCE)

MONBAZILLAC (BERGERAC – FRANCE)

VERY SWEET SHERRY (SOUTHWEST SPAIN)

WINE AND CREAM AND VANILLA

These desserts have a hidden danger for the wine-matcher: their creaminess and the vanilla are not as innocent as they seem. Honeyed wines are essential, otherwise such desserts will overwhelm the acidity of the wine's fruit, and thus what seemed like a smooth pud turns into a lumpy one. This curious effect would be heightened if, purely in the spirit of research, you sipped a very fruity Aussie Chardonnay, which in other circumstances would be considered extremely ripe and rich with a creamy pastry, and realized how numb the wine became as a result of the pud. So beware! A small glass of honeyed wine is marvellous with these styles of dessert, and can become a wonderful sauce for them. Try the Muscats from Quady in California.

Baked Alaska

SERVES 4–6

ALTHOUGH THIS LOOKS A COMPLICATED DESSERT, if you buy the ice-cream and sponge, and just make the meringue, you will get away with gastro murder. It looks impressive, especially when you put a match to it, but be careful because by dessert time dinner parties can get a bit raucous. The filling can vary according to the season or personal preferences. You could even mix some Christmas pudding with slightly softened vanilla ice-cream and flame it with brandy.

200G (7OZ) VANILLA ICE-CREAM | 200G (7OZ) RASPBERRY SORBET | 200G (7OZ) CASTER SUGAR | 100ML (3½FL OZ) EAU-DE-VIE FRAMBOISE | 150G (5½OZ) RASPBERRIES | ½ ROUND SPONGE CAKE FOR THE MERINGUE
3 EGG WHITES | 100G (3½OZ) CASTER SUGAR

1. Remove the ice-cream and sorbet from the freezer about 10 minutes before you assemble the Alaska.

Bring 200ml (7fl oz) of water and the sugar to the boil. Cool it a little, and add 40ml (1½fl oz) of the Eau-de-vie Framboise. Pour half the syrup into a processor, add a quarter of the raspberries, and blend. Then add another quarter of the raspberries to the sauce. Addd the remaining raspberries to the remaining sauce and keep aside. Cut the sponge into three discs 8mm (⅜-inch) thick. Put one layer onto an ovenproof serving dish, and brush it generously with some of the sauce. Spread the ice-cream over that, leaving about 2cm (¾-inch) of sponge around the edge. Spread the sorbet over the middle of the ice-cream, leaving the same gap of ice-cream on the edge. Put it into the freezer until firm, about 30–40 minutes.

2. Cut the two remaining slices of sponge in half, then cut three of the halves in half again. Cut the remaining half into a circle with a 10cm (4-inch) cutter, or use a sharp knife.

Remove the Alaska from the freezer and place the circle of sponge in the middle of the sorbet. Use the quarter pieces to cover the rest of the sorbet and ice-cream, overlapping the circle in the middle and meeting the piece of base sponge. This now protects the sorbet and ice-cream from melting when the Alaska is baked. Brush the top of the sponge generously with the sauce and return it to the freezer.

3. Meanwhile, whisk the egg whites until stiff. Add the sugar and continue whisking until really stiff and shiny. This should take about 3–4 minutes

Remove the Alaska from the freezer. Cover the ice-cream with the meringue, using a palette knife or a spatula to give a rough, natural effect. Return it to the freezer until required.

Preheat the oven to 200°C/400°F/ Gas mark 6. Bake the Alaska for 5–6 minutes until lightly coloured. Put the remaining Eau-de-vie Framboise into a saucepan and heat over a low flame. Take the Baked Alaska to the table. Carefully light the *eau-de-vie* with a match and pour over the Baked Alaska. Let the flames burn out, and serve it with the remaining raspberry sauce.

ICE-CREAM AND SORBET

Of all the ways of preserving food, ice-cream and sorbet probably get the most enjoyment and merits in the modern world, especially from kids. We probably don't even recognize them as ways of preserving, more as ways of life. As with chocolate, though, if you are not making it yourself, you need to read the back of the packet, or the wrapper for that matter. It's a quick fix on a hot summer's day, but you can make delicious ice lollies at home with just pure blended fruit. If you invest in an ice-cream maker, you can experiment with all sorts of combinations, even savoury ones. A sorbet can be a great palate cleanser after a heavy main course. Grown-ups can be treated to the potent concoction of a granita – made from wine, or another form of alcohol, mixed with a sugar syrup and frozen on a tray.

BAKED ALASKA

FLAMED EAU-DE-VIE, MY LIFE?! True, the flames quench the alcohol, but the flavour is retained and is intense (and also intensifies the raspberryness). Furthermore, any of the big, rich, treacly dessert wines (like the Matusalem recommended for the chocolate fondue with churros) somehow clash with the ice-cream. I would prefer something less oleaginous in my dessert wine glass here. For this reason, I am opting for... ah! I feel you anticipate me. You suspect I may be going to offer Eiswein? But, Eiswein (icewine), apart from being unsuitable for this dish, is an absurd German confection I have only ever experienced once as a great, toweringly great, worth-all-the-trouble-of-the-grower-getting-up-at-four-in-the-morning-on-Christmas-Day-to-pick-the-grapes great, wine once in my life. Indeed, I once had the singularly curious experience of tasting ninety-four icewines in a single day, and only one was truly fascinating.

So we must turn elsewhere. The wine I demand is Jurançon, a wine grown in the shadow of the Pyrénées in southwestern France. Jurançon, more than any other sweet white wine of the French, has a genteel spiciness to its richness. This spiciness, though subtle, is what we are after with this assertive dessert (fine examples are Domaine Cauhapé Quintessence, Domaine Bru-Baché l'Eminence, and Château Jolys late-harvest). And with an Alsatian Vendange Tardive Gewurztraminer we find the exuberance necessary to partner Mark's sumptuous, end-of-meal blow-out (names to look out for are Zind-Humbrecht, Weinbach, Hugel, and Kuentz-Bas).

WINES

JURANCON MOELLEUX (JURA – FRANCE)

VENDAGE TARDIVE GEWURZTRAMINER (ALSACE – FRANCE)

WINE AND ICE-CREAM AND SORBET

Wines to go with ice-creams and sorbets (the only exception is chocolate ice-cream) need to be delicate. A Muscat is good (from Alsace or Eastern Europe), a Gewurztraminer (young, from Alsace), or a young Feteasca from Hungary or Romania.

Mochachino Brûlée

SERVES 4

YOU'VE PROBABLY HAD ONE OF THESE CHOCOLATEY COFFEES, or at least seen it on the menu in a coffee chain. This is a more solid, eggy version – a bit like a chocaholic's crème brûlée with cream on top.

4 EGG YOLKS | 75G (2¾OZ) CASTER SUGAR | 250ML (9FL OZ) MILK | 250ML (9FL OZ) DOUBLE CREAM | 10G (¼OZ) GROUND COFFEE | 20G (¾OZ) COCOA POWDER | 100G (3½OZ) GOOD-QUALITY DARK CHOCOLATE, CHOPPED, OR CHOCOLATE BUTTONS
FOR THE TOPPING
75ML (2½FL OZ) MILK | 15G (½OZ) CASTER SUGAR | 1 SMALL EGG YOLK | 1TSP CORNFLOUR | 1TSP FLOUR | 125ML (4FL OZ) DOUBLE CREAM, SEMI-WHIPPED | 3TBSP BROWN SUGAR | A TABLESPOON OR SO OF COCOA POWDER

1. Preheat the oven to 150°C/300°F/ Gas mark 2. Whisk together the egg yolks and sugar. In a saucepan, mix the milk, cream, coffee, and cocoa powder, and bring to the boil. Add the chocolate and stir until dissolved. Add this to the egg mixture and stir well. Pour it through a fine sieve to remove the coffee grounds, and then into large cups, or tough glasses, to come halfway up the sides. Cover each cup with clingfilm, stand them in a bain-marie (a deep roasting tin part-filled with hot water) and cover with a sheet of foil. Bake for 40–50 minutes, or until they are firm. (If you're using small cups, 30 minutes will be enough.)

2. Remove the cups from the bain-marie and allow them to cool.

Now prepare the topping. Bring the milk to the boil. Mix together the sugar and egg yolk, then stir in the cornflour and flour. Pour the boiling milk onto the egg mixture and whisk together. Return the mixture to the pan and cook over a low heat for 1 minute, stirring constantly until it thickens. Pour it quickly into the blender and process until very smooth. Transfer the mixture to a bowl, and cover the actual cream with clingfilm to prevent it from forming a skin. When it is cold, fold in the semi-whipped cream.

3. Spoon the pastry cream mixture, about 2cm (¾-inch) thick, onto each brûlée, using the back of the spoon to smooth it. Sprinkle a thin layer of brown sugar on each, then caramelize with a blowtorch or by placing them under a hot grill for a few minutes. Stand the cups on their saucers, add teaspoon, and serve with a sprinkling of cocoa powder.

EGG-BASED DESSERTS
Eggs form a crucial part of dessert-making in the form of emulsifying, thickening, and decoration. There is no replacement for the egg in our dessert repertoire. When an egg is separated, we have two different essential ingredients: the yolk for enriching and thickening, and the white which can be whipped for meringue, or for lightening mousses and creams. Some of our most classic desserts are egg based: the crème brûlée or caramel would not exist without eggs; there would be no custard for our pies; and pavlova, whoever invented it, would not have got a look-in on the culinary map.

MOCHACHINO BRULEE

QUADY'S ELYSIUM FROM CALIFORNIA is one of those wines put on the planet specifically to go with desserts as extravagantly hedonistic as this one. Tokaj from Hungary must also be considered. With this latter wine, when you consider the delicacy with which the overripe, edging-towards-mouldy grapes were picked and slowly fermented (Tokajs can be so congealed that the yeast has a tough time gobbling up the sugar to convert it into alcohol, and some ferments last well over a year), the sums asked for the wines are far from exorbitant. In the absence of fresh goose liver, which the Magyars routinely wash down with Tokaj, you will find this pudding a splendid companion for this curious, marmalade-edged wine (pronounced "Tokay", spelt Tokaj on the bottle, and not to be confused with the Tokay Pinot Gris grape variety).

The name Tokaj is derived from a single village, Tokaj, in the northwest of Hungary, where nearly thirty villages now produce the wine, and it is a tradition going back to at least the middle of the seventeenth century. Its making involves the addition of concentrated must, and a 5 Puttonyos Tokaj, at the very least, is to be preferred for this pudding (a *puttonyos* is, in fact, a container used to carry the concentrated must, or *aszú*, and five additions mean that the wine will be particularly fine, complex, and rich). Such a wine is never at its best until at least ten years have passed since it was bottled (if you can find a twenty-year-old then so much the better).

This is in great contrast to the Quady wine, which is a modern phenomenon created by Andrew Quady in California's hot Central Valley in 1981 (though the winery dates from a little earlier). Without doubt, he makes California's lushest and most exciting sweet wines. This wine is excellent with many egg-based desserts, crème brûlées particularly, but with meringues I would suggest something more delicate: young Quarts-de-Chaume, made from the Chenin Blanc grape in the Loire.

WINE CHECKLIST

MUSCAT (CALIFORNIA – THE USA)

TOKAJ ASZU 5 PUTTONYOS (HUNGARY)

QUARTS-DE-CHAUME (LOIRE – FRANCE)

6
Cheese

BEFORE OR AFTER DESSERT? WHICH IS CORRECT, WE ASK OURSELVES? In France it's before dessert, but in the UK we tend to plonk it on the table after dessert and let guests get on with it. Well, to be perfectly honest, I'm not bothered which way round it goes, and I actually rather like the way the Italians sometimes serve it before the meal, just to put the cat among the pigeons. If you are serving cheese as a course, either before or after, the good old cheeseboard can be a frightfully boring affair, especially when you've just piled on it what's available from the local supermarket.

I much prefer to offer guests just a couple of well-sourced cheeses with a bit of a story, and preferably seasonable ones. I quite like to serve certain cheeses as a dish in their own right, such as a slice of Taleggio melted over some grilled focaccia or maybe over some stems of steamed sprouting broccoli.

I had one of my favourite cheeses in Aldeanueva del Camino in Spain. We had just visited Santo Domingo's pimento mill, and had lunch at the owner's hotel across the road. He served us Ibores goat's cheese, which is a semi-cured goat's cheese, simply sliced and melted on the plate, and dusted with semi-sweet pimento from across the road. It was perfect, and a fine example of how not to mess up ingredients.

Our knowledge of cheese is improving all the time, especially with specialist cheese shops popping up all over the country and making our cheeseboard selection more of an adventure. In fact, it seems that the cheesemonger has taken over from the poor old fishmonger.

I much prefer to offer guests just a couple of well-sourced cheeses with a bit of a story, and preferably seasonable ones.

Not so long ago we were blessed with mainly French and European cheeses and a small percentage of cheeses from the UK. There seems to have been a bit of a turnaround during this last decade, and all sorts of great producers from the UK are coming out of the woodwork. Many of them have been around for years, but only produced small quantities; some are diversifying and making new cheeses. I think we could proudly say that we are not far behind the French now when it comes to variety and quality. This statement may cause differing opinions, but why shouldn't we produce great cheeses when we have such great dairy products?

With this in mind, we should take our cheeses more seriously, and think more about what we serve them with. Cheese and biscuits is fine, but there are biscuits and biscuits. Certain cheeses are well partnered to a crisp salad of chicory, others to an oat biscuit and chutney. I generally find that the harder cheeses, like cheddar and Lancashire, are more suited to biscuits and chutney, and the softer cheeses, say a Stinking Bishop or a soft, Ragstone goat's cheese, are better off with a salad and crusty bread.

THERE WERE MANY REASONS WHY THE FAMOUS (OR SHOULD I SAY NOTORIOUS?) RED-WINE-AND-CHEESE PARTY BECAME SO POPULAR, not the least of them being that the two central ingredients got on so well together. There is an absolutely scientific explanation: certain cheeses, the hard ones almost invariably to be found at such get-togethers, coat the taste-buds with proteins which effectively nullify the coarse effects of the tannins in the wine, and so the austerity of what was often a cheap rustic red was mollified. It was, in short, improved by its liaison with the cheese, rather like rough, unshaven louts who melt and soften when they are confronted by an angelic female. This has led to one of the greatest, and most widely spread, misunderstandings in the field of wine and food matching. This is that red wine and cheese are made for one another, and that no other wine will do.

Certainly, a hard cheddar-type cheese can be superb with many Cabernet Sauvignons (those tannins again), but there is an abundance of other marriages arguably more exciting, more sensual, more thrillingly achievable. The first has to be sweet white wine and blue cheese. In the UK, there has grown up the tradition of vintage port and Stilton, and in some quarters they spoon out the middle of a ripe whole Stilton and pour in the port. I find this one of the most disgusting ideas on the planet, and I would rather consume smoked whole hedgehog with warm Retsina. Stilton does require a strong red, but Maury (from Catalan France) is better, as it is sweeter, and so is Amarone, from northeastern Italy. With other blue cheeses, Roquefort say, Monbazillac from the Dordogne in France is excellent, but so are the dessert whites

> In some quarters they spoon out the middle of a whole Stilton and pour in the port. I would rather consume smoked hedgehog with warm retsina.

made from the magnificent sounding Gros Manseng and Petit Manseng grapes in Béarn near the Pyrénées n France.

With soft white cheeses, an aromatic white wine, such as Tokay Pinot Gris or Gewurztraminer from Alsace, Loire moelleux or *demi-secs*, and Chenin Blancs from South Africa, can be splendid. With hard goat's cheese choose Shiraz, Cabernet Franc, Merlot from Hawke's Bay in New Zealand. With soft goat's cheese, go white again and pick New Zealand Pinot Gris, Cape and Aussie Chardonnays (splendid end to a meal such a pairing makes!), and Chilean Gewurztraminer.

I often keep the most powerful reds for the cheese board or cheese-style last course, which arrives following a light fish and salad course.

"So, Mark, what do you think about white wine and blue cheese?"

"I never would have believed, Malcolm, that my blue cheese and endive salad would go so faaaaaantastically with that Monbazillac of yours."

Baked Aubergine with Buffalo Mozzarella

SERVES 4

BUYING GOOD-QUALITY BUFFALO MOZZARELLA IS A MUST FOR THIS DISH. When you compare the creaminess of buffalo with industrial Mozzarella, you'll know what I mean. There are some rogue Mozzarellas around that have been pasteurized to lengthen the shelf life, but these are miles away from a quality, freshly made cheese. A good, trustworthy Italian deli should be able to give you exactly what you want.

SALT AND FRESHLY GROUND BLACK PEPPER | 1 AUBERGINE, CUT INTO FOUR 2CM (¾-INCH) **SLICES |** 1TSP **FRESH THYME LEAVES |** 2TBSP **OLIVE OIL | 2 BUFFALO MOZZARELLA WEIGHING ABOUT** 150G(5½ OZ) **EACH OR 4 SMALLER ONES | MALDON OR FLAKY SEA SALT**
FOR THE DRESSING
60ML (2¼FL OZ) **OLIVE OIL |** 1TBSP **CAPERS | 12 BLACK OLIVES, STONED AND QUARTERED |** 50G (1¼ OZ) **SEMI-DRIED OR SUN-BLUSHED TOMATOES, CUT INTO SAME SIZE PIECES AS THE OLIVES** | ½TBSP **BALSAMIC VINEGAR**

1. Preheat the oven to 200°C/400°F/ Gas mark 6. Season the slices of aubergine and scatter the thyme leaves over. Heat the olive oil in a heavy frying pan, and brown the aubergine slices on both sides, then cook them in the oven on a baking tray for 15–20 minutes. Leave to cool.

2. Meanwhile, mix together all the ingredients for the dressing. Place a slice of aubergine on a plate and cut each of the Mozzarellas into quarters for the large ones, or halves for the small. Arrange two pieces on each slice of aubergine. Spoon the dressing around and sprinkle with a little sea salt.

SOFT CHEESES

Soft cheeses fall into various categories, from those delicious, newly made goat's cheeses to flavourful, gooey, mature Brie. These soft cheeses are so versatile that in peak condition some of the triple crème ones are almost like natural fondues in themselves and need very little served with them except a simple green salad and some crusty bread.

Some of the classics, such as Brie, need no introduction, but there are some close contenders cropping up in the UK, like Ravensoak from Cheshire, and Milleens from Ireland.

FOLGÓRE
ROSSO
DENOMINAZIONE DI ORIGINE
CONTROLLATA
L. 0207

BAKED AUBERGINE WITH BUFFALO MOZZARELLA

THIS IS A MARVELLOUS ITALIAN DISH, AND IT REQUIRES A SWASHBUCKLING RED. We shall, then, visit Tuscany's San Gimignano, with its famous, absurd towers, and travel a little out of town to the Panizzi Estate. Giovanni Panizzi is the guv'nor here and he bought the estate in 1994 – thirty hectares of vines as well as olive trees – and enjoys nothing better than leaping aboard his Harley Davidson Heritage and inspecting his estate. San Gimignano Rosso Folgore has mild tannins with spice and coffee, and makes a fine friend to this dish (because it melds with the cheese yet doesn't overwhelm the aubergine).

But one other Italian wine clamours for inclusion here. More rewarding than the hyped Super Tuscans (*see* page 183) are wines made by Filippo Mazzei of Castello di Fonterutoli in Castellina in Chianti. A Fonterutoli Chianti Classico, perhaps comprising 90 per cent Sangiovese, 7 per cent Merlot, and 3 per cent of the local varieties Colorino, Mammolo, and Malvasia Nero, will be superb with this dish. So will the Ravenswood Vintners Blend Zinfandel from California, and Casa Lapostolle Cuvée Alexandre Merlot from Chile. The former is juicier, and really melts in the mouth (along with the cheese). The Merlot is more sedate, and makes itself more at home with the aubergines. Either wine makes a thoughtful companion for the dish.

WINE CHECKLIST

SAN GIMIGNANO ROSSO (TUSCANY – ITALY)

CHIANTI CLASSICO (TUSCANY – ITALY)

ZINFANDEL (CALIFORNIA – USA)

MERLOT (CHILE)

Baked Vacherin Mont d'Or

SERVES 3–4

VACHERIN IS SUCH AN INDULGENT CHEESE AND ONE OF MY FAVOURITES, HOT OR AU NATUREL. It's made in the Alps, but the Swiss now have exclusive rights to call theirs Mont d'Or, whereas previously Mont d'Or could be made either side of the northwestern Swiss/French border. This cheese is in season during the winter months from early October and, served at room temperature, has a unique, velvety texture.

Vacherin comes in its own little wooden box that allows it to continue maturing, so the riper it gets the more liquid it becomes. The box is a perfect vessel for baking the cheese in. Result: fondue, naturally. Yes, fondue. You must know that it's wildly fashionable again. Couples getting married now probably have a fondue set on their wedding list, but anyone who married ten years ago probably got a sandwich-maker instead. This doesn't really need a recipe – or a fondue set – but here's how.

1. Take an individual Vacherin, which weighs about 500g (1lb 2oz), and bake it for 15–20 minutes at 180°C/350°F/ Gas mark 4. Serve with slices of toasted baguette or leaves of endive. There you are, fondue without the fuss.

CHEESE AND HOT DISHES

Serving cheese hot is not such a bad thing. In fact, some cheeses were naturally designed to be served hot. Raclette, Taleggio, and Vacherin are sheer indulgence, and the likes of Vacherin and Camembert can even be baked in the oven in the neat little wooden boxes they have been matured in. Back home here we have the good old Welsh Rarebit, which is traditionally made with Caerphilly, but often gets made with cheddar and other hard cheeses. Unlike similar dishes overseas, it gets served as a savoury course or snack – often not as a cheese course at all.

BAKED VACHERIN MONT D'OR

A CHILLED BOTTLE OF TWENTY-YEAR-OLD TAWNY PORT provides a superb contrast of acids, textures, and temperatures to this marvellously simple dish. Tawny is often associated with club bores, collapsible old men in uncollapsible old leather chairs taking pre-lunch gulps of the stuff as they struggle with *The Times* crossword. Nevertheless, it is a superb wine, unjustly neglected, and wildly delicious, and gamey (rather like this dish). It is important to get a tawny which has twenty years on the label, though whether all the wine in the bottle will be that age is moot, for tawny is a blend of ports, aged so that it has acquired a tawny character and lost the crimson bloom of youth. What I adore about a wine like this is its indomitability: it is so much of itself; it is incorrigible, except with food when it learns how to become yielding and characterful. Such a wine offers an undertone of roasted nuts along with its delicate fruitiness, often recalling dried fruit (pears, plums, apricots), yet it is never outlandishly or indeed monodimensionally sweet. It is wonderful with this dish. The best names to look for are Sandeman, Niepoort, Fonseca, and Ramos-Pinto, though Cockburn, Croft, Delaforce, Dow's, Graham's, Noval, Taylor's, and Warre are also good.

However, perhaps you crave a red wine with this dish? To this end, let us bypass Chianti Classico and travel to the adjacent region of the Maremma. In 1997, the Mazzei family of Chianti extended its horizons by buying the Tenuta Belguardo Estate, some ten miles from the coast in the Parco dell'Uccellina in Maremma (which is in the Grosseto province). This is not Chianti, but the Sangiovese grape predominates along with Cabernet Sauvignon, Merlot, and some local Alicante. Tenuta Belguardo Morellino di Scansano is the Mazzei wine I would choose from here to accompany that Vacherin. They keep one another in beautiful company.

WINE CHECKLIST

TAWNY PORT, 20-YEAR-OLD (PORTUGAL)

SANGIOVESE/CABERNET SAUVIGNON/MERLOT/ALICANTE BLEND (MAREMMA, TUSCANY – ITALY)

Endive and Roquefort Salad with Toasted Walnuts

SERVES 4

BELGIUM ENDIVE, OR CHICORY, CAN BE A LITTLE BORING ON ITS OWN IN A SALAD, unless it has a really good mustardy vinaigrette, or this classic Roquefort dressing. The walnuts give it a delicious savoury crunch in a croûton sort of fashion.

4 MEDIUM HEADS OF BELGIUM ENDIVE | **30G (1OZ) WALNUT HALVES** | **1TSP OLIVE OIL** |
MALDON SEA SALT
FOR THE DRESSING
60ML (2¼FL OZ) EXTRA-VIRGIN OLIVE OIL MIXED WITH 60ML (2¼FL OZ) VEGETABLE OIL |
1TBSP WHITE WINE VINEGAR | **1TSP DIJON MUSTARD** | **100G (3½OZ) ROQUEFORT CHEESE** |
SALT AND FRESHLY GROUND BLACK PEPPER

1. With a knife, trim the roots from the endive and separate the leaves, removing any that are discoloured. Wash and dry them in a salad spinner or colander.

2. Preheat the grill and place the walnuts onto some foil on the grill tray. Drizzle with the olive oil, season with the sea salt, and grill until lightly toasted. Leave to cool.

3. To make the dressing, blend all the ingredients, reserving 80g (2¾oz) of the cheese, in a liquidizer until smooth, and season with a little salt and pepper, if necessary. Serve the salad leaves tossed in the dressing, with the walnuts and remaining cheese scattered on top.

BLUE CHEESES

The uniqueness of blue cheeses sets them apart from their soft, hard, and mature cousins. They are a breed of their own, and, on the whole, are quite delicious, but they have an acquired and sophisticated following.

Stilton and Roquefort seem to take the lead worldwide as the kings of the blues, but the fast-growing cheese industry is certainly showing some close competition. Some of my favourites are Jersey blue, Yorkshire blue, and Cashel blue. They all have different characters, from yellow and buttery to dense blue with a tang of bitter-sweetness.

ENDIVE AND ROQUEFORT SALAD WITH TOASTED WALNUTS

THIS DISH IS DOMINATED BY A VERY STRONG, TANGY CHEESE of infinitely generous deliciousnesss but also an extreme narrowness of choice when it comes to the wine. A sweet white wine is ideal, and a Monbazillac from Bergerac would be my first choice. This is because, although they are honeyed, the best examples exhibit a waxy richness which happily co-exists with the uncompromising tanginess of the Roquefort. The best producers are Domaine de l'Ancienne Cure (Cuvée Abbaye), Château Fonmourgues, Château La Borderie, Château Haut-Bernasse, Clos Fontindoule, Château Le Fagé, and Château Tirecul la Gravière.

Those are my first choices. But what of other sweet white wines? I cannot pretend that only Monbazillac works with Roquefort, and indeed that isn't so, but do not forget the other ingredients: the bitter endive and the walnuts, which other, carelessly chosen, sweet white wines might drown. Certainly, the Jurançon *moelleux* chosen to go with the Baked Alaska – Domaine Cauhapé Quintessence, Domaine Bru-Baché l'Eminence and Château Jolys – would be interesting partners for this dish.

WINE CHECKLIST

MONBAZILLAC (BERGERAC – FRANCE)

JURANCON MOELLEUX (BEARN – FRANCE)

WINE AND BLUE CHEESES
There are two things that always stagger me about professional chefs. One is their ability to work angelically in Hell (which a restaurant kitchen always is, though its inmates are not always as angelically unruffled as Mr Hix when they run things). The other is their surprise when I say how much I love sweet white wine with blue cheeses. Many a chef seems never to heard of this sublime pairing, and one, who shall be nameless, was convinced I was having him on until I presented him with the evidence.

Parmesan-Fried Courgette

SERVES 4–6

WE SERVE THESE AT DAPHNE'S IN CHELSEA, and they are often ordered as a pre-dinner snack with the bread rather than as a vegetable dish – which is exactly what I suggest you do with them. The easiest way to shred these is with a slicing gadget called a mandolin.

2–3 MEDIUM-SIZED COURGETTES | VEGETABLE OR CORN OIL, FOR FRYING | 3–4TBSP PLAIN FLOUR, SEASONED | 3–4TBSP FINELY GRATED PARMESAN | ABOUT 100ML (3½FL OZ) MILK | SALT AND FRESHLY GROUND BLACK PEPPER

1. Cut the courgettes into 10cm (4-inch) lengths, and shred them finely with a knife, or with a shredding attachment on a mandolin or a food processor. Heat about 8cm (3¼ inch) of oil to 160–180°C (325–350°F) in a large thick-bottomed saucepan or an electric deep-fat fryer.

Have three bowls or shallow dishes ready: one with the seasoned flour mixed with the Parmesan, the second with the milk, and the third for the finished courgettes. This gets a bit messy, by the way.

2. Use your left hand to coat some of the courgettes in the flour mixture, shaking off any excess, then drop them into the milk and give them a stir with your right hand until coated. Remove them from the milk, shaking off any excess, then drop them back into the flour. Dry your right hand off and mix the courgettes well in the flour mix until they are well coated. Transfer them to the third bowl.

Repeat with the rest of the courgettes.

3. Fry the courgettes a handful or so at a time, stirring and turning them in the fat so that they cook and colour evenly. Remove with a slotted spoon onto a plate covered with kitchen paper, and repeat with the rest of the courgettes. Lightly season and serve immediately.

HARD CHEESES

These can be pretty hard-core for the tame and safe cheese-lovers. Even cheddar fans used to eating the mild and medium cheddars will turn their noses up at extra mature truckles, which become almost Parmesan- and aged-Pecorino-like, and take on an acidity that perhaps only an educated palate can appreciate. In the UK a good old chutney or pickle is the perfect match for a mature hard cheese before or after dessert, but in Italy you are more likely to be presented with a chunk of Parmesan for your starter or as an aperitif.

PARMESAN-FRIED COURGETTE

I WOULD MAKE THE ASSUMPTION THAT THIS DISH WILL NOT BE EATEN BY ITSELF, although it is sufficiently delicious and wholesome to be so served. It would accompany some lamb chops perhaps, or stuffed peppers, or indeed anything you fancy. However, though this puts the wine waiter in a somewhat uncertain state of mind, we shall discount it and recommend a wine on the basis of courgettes and Parmesan alone. A good, sturdy Chianti springs to mind immediately – earthy, proud, deeply berried – but such wines are, I find, increasingly difficult to find with any weight and true wit (without coming attached to a hefty price tag). However, some of the wines from Cantina del Castello di Brolio are worth investigating if your pocket is capacious. A wine like Brolio Casalferro, an 80 per cent Sangiovese/20 per cent Merlot blend, in any of the vintages from 1999 on, has class, though it does not come cheap. Casalferro is also excellent from the 2000 vintage on (again it is not cheap). There is a motto attached to the Brolio coat of arms – "nothing without pain" – so the prices there are bound to be as steep as the ascent to the ancient Tuscan castle itself.

Thanks to human factors like vanity and egotism, however, we find in Tuscany much of the same lack of overall brilliance that characterizes the Burgundy region in France. Buying Tuscan wines, then, can be a lottery (apart from the producers named in this book, whom I have found reliable). The so-called Super Tuscan red Tignanello, made by the most influential Italian international wine corporation, Antinori, oozes charm, texture, and aristocratic richness, but so do Italian wines costing a quarter of that price. Sassicaia has become no less of a trophy wine, to be avoided except when offered free. Le Stanze del Poliziano is to be preferred (the 2000 vintage was sumptuous). This is also a Super Tuscan, it has to be said, from Montepulciano, but Federico Carletti makes this Bordeaux blend, typically 65 per cent Cabernet Sauvignon, 30 per cent Merlot, and 5 per cent Sangiovese, into one of the most worthwhile of such wines. Its cost is not a silly amount to spend, but it is a stupendous amount of liquid to drink, especially with this dish. It displays coffee and gently spiced berries of charm and great persistence.

WINE CHECKLIST

CHIANTI (TUSCANY – ITALY)

CABERNET SAUVIGNON/ MERLOT/SANGIOVESE BLEND (MONTEPULCIANO, TUSCANY – ITALY)

WINE AND HARD CHEESES

With hard and aged cheeses, there is great concentration of acidic richness and this affects the choice of wine. A mature cheddar is fine with a Chilean Cabernet Sauvignon, but with harder, riper, older cheeses a more robust wine is required. My usual habit is to reach for a bottle of ten-year-old tawny port.

Caramelized Onion and Goat's Cheese Tart

SERVES 4

THIS IS A GREAT SAVOURY LUNCH SNACK OR DINNER-PARTY DISH that you can prepare in advance and just pop in the oven at the last minute. It would also make a great picnic or lunch-box snack.

400G (14OZ) PUFF PASTRY, ROLLED TO ABOUT ⅓CM (⅛-INCH) THICK | 4 LARGE ONIONS, THINLY SLICED | 1TSP CHOPPED THYME LEAVES | 1TBSP OLIVE OIL | SALT AND FRESHLY GROUND BLACK PEPPER | 50G (1¾OZ) BUTTER | 100G (3½OZ) SOFT GOAT'S CHEESE, BROKEN INTO PIECES

1. Cut the pastry into 4 circles about 12cm (4½ inch) in diameter. Prick them all over with a fork to prevent the pastry from rising too much, then put them on a baking tray. Rest the pastry for 45 minutes in the refrigerator. Meanwhile, gently cook the onions and thyme in the oil on a low heat with the lid on for 4–5 minutes until they begin to soften, giving them a good stir every so often.

2. Season with salt and pepper, add the butter, and continue cooking the onions for about 10 minutes with the lid on until they begin to get really soft. Remove the lid, turn the heat up a little, and cook for a further 5 minutes or until they begin to colour. Preheat the oven to 160°C/320°F/Gas mark 3.

3. Bake the pastry for 7 minutes, and remove from the oven. Turn up the oven to 200°C/400°F/Gas mark 6.

Spread the onion mixture onto the pastry. Arrange the cheese on top, and cook for another 8–10 minutes until the cheese melts. Serve hot or cold.

STRONG CHEESES

I must say I'm not a great lover of really sticky, pongy cheeses. The great thing with cheeses is that there is something out there for every individual taste.

Even if you don't particularly like cheese, you could easily eat young, soft, creamy goat's cheese without a problem. The likes of Roquefort actually tell you in their name that they have that certain strength, but without knowing that you could be in for a surprise. One of our great cheeses is Stinking Bishop, made by Charles Martell, where he washes his Single Gloucester in perry – the pear equivalent of cider. The end result is absolutely fantastic, as the rind develops a rather pleasant mould that penetrates into the cheese.

CARAMELIZED ONION AND GOAT'S CHEESE TART

A WINE TO GO WITH A TART? THIS IS A SERIOUS SUBJECT. A deeply, deeply serious subject. You think I jest? When I was, some years ago now, approached to be wine editor of the UK edition of *Cosmopolitan* magazine I leapt at the opportunity to develop a new readership which the editors surely understood did not take matters vinous too seriously. How wrong I was. My recommendation that Australian Chardonnay, owing to the nature of its secondary malolactic fermentation, could promote multiple orgasms was struck out by the editor on grounds of taste. Further prunings followed over future months, and I began to wonder just for whom it was the editors assumed I was writing.

The parting of the ways came when I was asked to contribute suggestions one month as to the wines which could accompany the food editor's quiches. The first line of my submitted column read: "This month's column was a doddle to write as the extensive research required has been going for years. Between my two marriages I spent years finding wines to go with tarts." The editor said the second line was outrageously sexist, and insisted on its removal. Shortly after this, I was removed myself – fired. But I have never lost my lust for tarts, and Mark knows how to concoct a tasty one.

It is a delight, therefore, to recommend the wines to go with it, and the list is headed by Chilean Merlot and Chilean Merlot/Cabernet Sauvignon, along with Argentine Malbec. These wines will do nothing for your sex life, but they will provide a sveltely textured, aromatically berried richness of fruit which is perfect with this tart. Names to look for? Well, top of the list must come Cuvée Alexandre from Casa Lapostolle along with Montes, followed by Viña La Rosa, Concha y Toro's Casillero del Diablo, Erráruriz and Casa Lapostolle (without the Cuvée Alexandre dimension). Zapata Catena Malbec (Argentina) is also a terrific wine with this tart.

WINE CHECKLIST

MERLOT (CHILE)

MERLOT/CABERNET SAUVIGNON BLEND (CHILE)

MALBEC (ARGENTINA)

STRONG CHEESES

It is often easy to be fooled by the pungent aroma of a cheese into assuming it is equally robustly flavoured. An eloquent case in point is Münster, from Alsace. It smells like the inside of a footballer's boot after a hard game. It tastes as delicate as an angel's kiss. And the wine to drink with it is a young local Gewurztraminer. The result is a mouth-watering marriage of stunning perfumes.

Index

Page numbers in **bold** indicate main entries; those in *italic* indicate illustrations and/or captions

Acknowledgements

FROM MARK

My biggest influence in my early days in the business was my college lecturer Lawrie Mills. He pointed me in the right direction and encouraged me to follow his career path by training in west end hotels. I consequently ended up working at the Grosvenor House hotel and the Dorchester under Anton Mossiman. Working for Jeremy King and Chris Corbin at Le Caprice was a big learning curve and that really polished my restaurant knowledge and I learnt what the customer really wanted.

Thanks to Malcolm and to Jason for those entertaining photo shoots, and to the wonderful team at Mitchell Beazley – in particular Juanne for doing the ironing! – and copy-editor Vanessa Kendell. And lastly to Kevin from St John restaurant in London who helped me out in the kitchen.

FROM MALCOLM

I would like to dedicate this book to RJJ, R.I.P., for driving the first marriage vehicle (MG).

This book would not exist without Commissioning Editor Hilary Lumsden. Her faith in it has never wavered as the two authors stuffed themselves and quaffed, missed deadlines, and generally argued the toss. Yasia Williams, Executive Art Editor, must be thanked for her devotion and good cheer. Juanne Branquinho, Managing Editor, likewise. Vanessa Kendell endured hours of frantic copy-editing, battling a rough sea of foreign labelling, and never got tetchy once. Grade Design Consultants, who designed the book, has done an exemplary job. With regard to the natty cover, we would also like to acknowledge Tim Foster's decisive input. And lastly, there is Jason Lowe whose Contax camera has clicked so elegantly.

FROM MITCHELL BEAZLEY

Mitchell Beazley would like to thank all the contributors for supplying the wines and Schott Zwiesel for supplying the glasses and decanters (except those featured on pages 7, 31, 64, 28, 88, 136, 146, 155, and 176) for the photoshoot.